Year of
Living Deeply

Year of Living Deeply

A Memoir of 1969

Robert Atkinson

50th Anniversary Edition

ONE VOICE
PRESS

WILMETTE, ILLINOIS

One Voice Press
401 Greenleaf Avenue, Wilmette, Illinois 60091
Copyright © 2019 Robert Atkinson
All rights reserved. Published 2019
Printed in the United States of America on acid-free paper ∞

22   21   20   19   4   3   2   1

ISBN 13: 978-1-61851-134-8

Cover design by Jamie Hanrahan
Book design by Patrick Falso

Cover photos (clockwise from upper left): Jimmy Collier, Pete Seeger, and Don McLean at a local sloop festival; the author; the author with Pete Seeger at the tiller; Arlo and Jackie Guthrie at their farm with Jack Elliott; the cabin in the woods; the sloop Clearwater at South Street Seaport.

For
My parents & grandparents

For
[faint handwritten dedication, illegible]

"For the son who has grown really to know the father, the agonies of the ordeal are readily borne; the world is no longer a vale of tears but a bliss-yielding, perpetual manifestation of the Presence."

—Joseph Campbell, *The Hero With a Thousand Faces*

Contents

Contents

Foreword

There is a new kind of sacred literature emerging into the collective mindscape. It does not follow the canons or articles of faith of any known religious tradition—or literary tradition, for that matter—but rather emerges out of a contemporary life, lived under the open skies of metaphysical exploration. In this emergent genre, the individual finds his or her way to a personal gnosis, a unique biographical penetration of the mystery of life and a nugget, a personal gem of wisdom is extracted. It is usually both personal and transpersonal—a paradox. If the encounter with experience is done with integrity, there is a flowing forth of wisdom from a transcendent Source, something is touched in our own experience of living, and it may be shared with others.

This remarkable journal begins in an early life, as a sensitive boy struggles with a flaw—a speech impediment. His voice lacks inner authority it seems, and thus a quest is initiated. He begins listening to a voiceless voice that speaks within his own soul—guiding him. He takes the advice and finds himself on a timeless adventure. As Joseph Campbell said, "If you follow your bliss, doors will open for you that you didn't even know were there."

Bob Atkinson finds himself sniffing down the corridors of the possible—synchronicities begin to unfold all around him, and he realizes he is in a subtle game of discovery with the materials of his life. His period of becoming is well-synchronized to that of a generation engaged in a creative rethinking of the world . . . the *sixties*, magic times, magic places.

Atkinson's daimon leads him to the launching of the ship *Clearwater*, a noble experiment in the dawning of a new consciousness, in which environmentalism, humanism, and a new spirituality seemed to be breaking simultaneously into the mindscape of the culture. The *Clearwater* was destined to become famous—the heart of local festivals up and down the Hudson River, and the inauguration of a focal movement toward clean water and air. (It is important to realize just how influential that time and those events were, as we now enjoy a scenic Hudson one can swim and fish in—and the *Clearwater* still plies the river, spreading joy, raising ecological awareness.)

Atkinson's contact with Pete Seeger and Arlo Guthrie, and the galaxy of talented visionaries around them, lends a mythic air to the landscape of the Hudson Valley—an epiphany seems to hide behind every rock, and in every glade; and the local myth of Rip Van Winkle, the ever-awakening man, becomes a parable of the awakening human soul.

Atkinson lives, first like an anchorite-mystic in a rustic cabin in the woods, then takes lodging in a monastery to weather out the New York winter. It seems a place of genuine wisdom and charity where the homeless are succored. Here through dream and vision, our hero finally seems to come into his own as a spiritual pilgrim, walking his path with new devotion and strength. His insights are not unfamiliar to students of the Perennial Philosophy—the path is based on the cultivation of love—and a faith in the guidance that keeps surprising us with its appropriateness. As the journey becomes decidedly more mythic, Atkinson meets an appropriate guide—Campbell himself—through a surprising series of synchronicities.

Joseph Campbell did for Robert Atkinson what he did for many a young writer or creative artist: set him firmly on the path to himself. Not through directing him, this way or that, but by pointing to the landmarks which have been left by human heroes on their parallel paths since time out of mind. "Peace, traveler, only look at the signs around you, and follow the burning in your own heart. Then your feet will not stray."

The denouement of this lovely story of one man's journey to selfhood comes through another synchronicity whereby he is hired by his own alma mater to teach a course in the life-wisdom transmitted by the lyrics of folk and popular music. A more apt invitation could not have been found, in the light of Atkinson's recent journey. Now his speech impediment is overcome, not because he has strengthened his vocal cords, but because he has tempered his soul. The authentic voice begins to emerge effortlessly—and what it speaks is soul-lore. Thus the transpersonal and the personal are woven together, and Atkinson realized the import of Campbell's parting words to him: "The archetypes of your experience represent your most reliable truth. Integrate them into your daily living. Transmit their meaning to others."

This indeed is what Professor Robert Atkinson has done in his career since the extraordinary life-transformative period that forms the main substance of this beautiful little book: teach fearlessly out of his own authentic experience—and with an essential voice. Listen to it, and you will find it full of wisdom and poetry—and an empowerment of your own mythic journey.

Stephen Larsen,
New Paltz, NY

Preface to the 50th Anniversary Edition

Writing this memoir has been about living into the mystery of time, trying to understand how time can be both fleeting and changeless at the same time, and how both aspects can even sometimes merge into a hidden wholeness.

One thing that is now even clearer with time is that this period in my life has made everything else possible since. Without these experiences, I have no idea who I would have become. With them, everything since this time in my life makes perfect sense.

This series of events and experiences, fifty years ago when so much else was changing everywhere so quickly, was a perfect alignment of forces, circumstances, and opportunities that all added up to become the foundation—and framework—for the rest of my life. I've pretty much always been aware of this, but can always use more time to fully digest, integrate, and appreciate this fact.

How could I have ever predicted that a decision I made about a master's thesis topic, in a program I came to only after a quick cross-country trip for another master's program that wasn't quite right for me, would have led to a chance meeting with Pete Seeger, who not only became a mentor but who invited me to sail on the maiden voyage of the sloop *Clearwater* up the Hudson River, which put me in just the right place at the right time to attend Woodstock?

And, how could I have ever imagined that that fall I would have lived in a cabin in the woods by the river, where I would be able to reflect deeply on the meaning of nature unfolding around me, and that a random visit to the city one night would have led to another chance meeting, this time with Joseph Campbell, who became the other mentor I needed just then to help me make sense of all that I was living at that time?

Or, how could I have known that not being able to stay the winter in the cabin would have led me to a nearby Franciscan monastery where I was given a cell of my own to live in, where I learned from the friars about a sacred tradition all new to me?

And, I could have never predicted then that from there I'd return to the college I had graduated from three years earlier to teach a course all of this had been preparing me for, and which completed a transformative cycle in my life I would have never expected.

The thing about this fiftieth anniversary edition is that it makes even clearer how absolutely vital it is for everyone to undertake their own independent investigation of reality. It doesn't matter if one is already an elder, in the prime of life, or just entering adulthood; our time calls for abandoning a blind and unexamined acceptance of what might have been common in the past.

Our needs and circumstances are very different now; indeed, our very survival depends upon shifting our thinking, our vision, from a perspective of what might be best or most desirable for us individually, or even as a nation, to what will best sustain and contribute to our collective wellbeing on this fragile planet that is our homeland.

We need, desperately and with the greatest urgency, to investigate our own inner reality—where we've come from, what we're meant to be doing here, and where we're going from here—along with the outer reality we share with each other in this vast and miraculous Creation in order to discover our role, purpose, and responsibility in helping to sustain it all.

When we each do this on our own, we will discover the same thing, that reality is one indivisible whole, that all separation is an illusion, and that this understanding may be the only thing that will unite us as a human family and with all other life around us.

It is my hope even fifty years after these experiences changed and redirected my life that their universality and timelessness may serve a role in some small way to redirect our collective vision toward what we all have in common.

Preface

This memoir originally came forth rather spontaneously as an epic poem, in four parts reflecting the four seasons, at the culmination of a series of serendipitous adventures. But this process included numerous drafts, revisions, and genres, providing me with much opportunity for reflection, and growing amazement at all that happened then.

I was a bit reluctant to finally give birth to such a personal expression until I realized that in some mysterious way, my experience is more than just mine. This time in my life is certainly the most profound of transitional moments, a time of inner preparation, and maturing into roles yet to be defined. But beyond this, the things that happened to me are archetypal experiences that are meant to connect us to each other. I tell my story that you may see in it something of your own.

I have consciously chosen to emphasize my internal understandings of the unique external events and circumstances of my life, and their meanings for me, rather than fully develop the concreteness of those events and surroundings that helped facilitate these understandings. In so doing, I hope to more closely approach the universal in all our stories.

I ask, as might Walt Whitman or Carl Jung, my models of autobiographical reflection, that you suspend your expectation of what a memoir is, of where the details and texture should be, so that you may be able to follow where my reflections took me. That is because what I have written here is as much an allegorical memoir, which by nature shifts the focus from the external happenings themselves to the internal interpretations of what they mean. This transformative time in my life is for me best expressed as something other than what was in plain sight. Understanding the significance of what was hidden within the events, and seeking to lift up this essence, has made the writing and rewriting of my story for so long a labor I have gladly borne.

I would like to express my gratitude to my grandparents, my parents, and all the friends I met along the way, especially Richard Orton, Pete and Toshi Seeger, Jack Elliott, Gordon Bok, Don McLean, Allan Aunapu, Judy Kossin, Arlo and Jackie Guthrie, Eric and Emily Knud-Hansen, Joseph Campbell, Father Jeremiah, Brother Joe, Brother Joachim, and Dr. Robert Cooke. I would also like to thank those who have taken the time to read and comment on my story at various points in its evolution: Stanwood Cobb, Marzieh Gail, Bahiyyih Nakhjavani, Anne Gordon, Beverly Jennison, Cynthia Atkinson, Stephen Larsen, Ellen Kleiner, Stephany Evans, Christina Baldwin, Michael Parkin, Kathy Krug, Jennifer Meader, and Michael Brady. I am especially grateful to Terry Cassiday and Nat Yogachandra for their commitment to this project, and Alex McGee, Bahhaj Taherzadeh, and Christopher Martin for their superb editorial assistance.

Prologue

I am an only child. Yet like every child, something within me yearns for union. Parades of celebration filled the streets soon after I was born, my mother told me. Not for me, but for the end of one era and the beginning of another. This was when the first atomic bomb turned a world at war into a nuclear village. But peace was elusive, and without realizing, my life became a quest to find it.

It was much later, when ageless archetypes began to emerge from deep within me, that I gradually became aware of the story my life was telling. This is when I realized that my story is much like many others. I shall explain.

I grew up near the potato fields, woods, and waters of eastern Long Island, in the middle ground between my mother (outgoing, responsive, imaginative, and persistent) and my father (quiet, gentle, practical, and easygoing). Living within this dialectic has for me been both a challenge and an opportunity.

When I was three, we moved to a new one-story home in a neighborhood off Main Street in a small farming community with its share of ethnic neighborhoods, from which I would find many of my friends.

My mom and I spent much of our time at home while my dad worked for the state department of agriculture. She was the one who very early set me on a spiritual path—one I am still on today—by reading children's Bible stories to me.

My dad worked around the house when he was not at the office. He kept the lawn and yard in top shape, and inside helped finish a game room in the basement and my bedroom in the attic.

I remember walking down our block to Main Street when I was five or six. I'd try to time it so I'd get to the corner where the noon whistle blew just as my dad drove by on his way home for lunch. He would always stop and give me a ride back. I looked forward to these outings; they gave me a wonderful feeling, a little freedom at one end, a lot of security at the other.

My dad and I did many things together, mostly sports. We played catch often, and he was the manager of my Little League team. Because he was always there for me, I felt loved.

My parents provided me with everything I needed, and more, but the one thing I had to find on my own was my voice, which turned out to be a long and painful process. I didn't know why, but I was slow to speak. Around the age of three, I began to stutter.

Once I started school, the stuttering increased. It was frustrating and embarrassing. Sometimes, perhaps most of the time, I could speak fine. But on other occasions, I would do everything possible to avoid the pain of being unable to express myself.

There were certain words and sounds I could not articulate—it was as though they were blocked within me. I would take time to think of other words I could say in their place. Sometimes this worked; other times I got stuck when the word I wanted just wouldn't come. I could hear myself say it in my mind, but I would stammer, trying my hardest to get it out, only to end up stuttering my way through it. In time I opted for silence and let my voice go unheard.

My parents were concerned and supportive. They spoke to my teachers. They consulted doctors. But there was nothing anyone could do to prevent the stuttering. Not even my kindergarten teacher, a great ally, could lessen the impact the embarrassment had on me.

I wondered why my voice was trapped within me. Something mysterious kept me from saying all that I could think.

This challenge went on until I was about nine. Then, gradually, my stuttering began to let up. Over the years, it became less noticeable to others, but I continue to carry its effects with me.

Long after I could speak more comfortably, I remained quiet, and often stayed in the background. Looking back on what it was like for me in high school, it now seems as if I was sleepwalking through most of it. Even though I had many friends and I participated in sports and other events, an important part of me remained dormant, unexpressed.

Everyone has their own burden, their own challenge in life that is unique to them. Childhood stuttering, and how I viewed my world because of that, has been my struggle. Though clearly not as severe or dramatic as obstacles faced by some, this presented enough of a hurdle for me that it propelled me down a path of self-discovery long before I was aware of it.

When my grandmother came to live with us for several months each year after my grandfather died, around the time I was nine, my stuttering seemed to lessen. Perhaps this timing was more than a coincidence.

I had been intrigued by both my grandparents for some time. My grandfather was an individualistic, freethinking dentist; my grandmother was a gentle, quiet woman, committed to her spiritual life. Their thoughtfulness and love of truth captured my attention early.

My parents, educated only through high school, seemed wise beyond their learning; my grandparents, with their unquenchable desire for knowledge, became models of lifelong learning for me.

When my grandmother was with us, she modeled for me the life of the spirit. I observed her often, reading silently from the Bible and *The Upper Room*. Her daily practice of devotion was something new to me then. Yet I must have sensed that the ageless verities were a source of nourishment to her thirsty soul, bringing her closer to God, for I saw clearly that she led a life of gratitude. She spent a good deal of her time doing what she cared most about, and she acted upon her convictions every day with gentle kindness. Her soft words carried the power of a tender, loving spirit.

I don't think I knew it then, but her resolve, her sense of direction, her assurance, and her commitment made a difference to my soul, too. Her quietude and steadfastness invited the extraordinary into her life, and quite possibly into mine, as well.

My grandmother lived what my soul yearned for. Her actions planted the seed of hope within me, showing me in her direct but subtle way that I could rely on the signs that came my way, that there was nothing to fear, and, best of all, that I could listen to myself. She also kept alive my wonder, kindling my curiosity for things seen and unseen, and awakening within me a reverence for the mysteries of life.

One day while she was with us, I was sitting on my bed looking out the window, and a "voice" came to me. I could not tell if it was speaking from within me or from somewhere else. The "voice" said, "Some day *you* will know God."

Although I did not understand the meaning of these words, I did begin to get a sense at that moment that this "voice" had something in store for me. It felt like an early warning for something I needed to be on the lookout for.

Many years later, after high school, college, and a year of graduate school, I finally heard from that voice again, during the summer of my twenty-fourth year. I was drawn to people, elders especially, whom I felt had personal wisdom to share about life.

I followed my desire to learn how and why people like my grandmother lived their lives the way they did. While studying folklore in graduate school, I conducted a life story interview with a traditional farmer-singer from the Catskill Mountains. Listening intently to his voice, I began to understand his life as he understood it himself. This allowed me even more of a glimpse of how I wanted my story to unfold.

Then, one day, my life took a turn I had not anticipated. Without much warning, I lost a relationship I thought would last forever. I was alone, discouraged and anxious. The best I could do was turn my gaze inward, seek a deeper meaning in my life, and try to find my inner voice.

I had listened to the voices of others long enough. They had much to tell me, but this was my opportunity to consciously search for where I wanted to be, what I wanted to do, and not settle for where others thought I should fit in the world.

My quest to find my own middle ground—where body, mind, and spirit would merge as one—began when hearing and speaking with my *own* voice became foremost.

This is my story; it is not a history, or a scientific recounting, but the story of my heart. It is a story of the truth that came forth from within me after having lived deeply through a time of great change, a time in my life when only these things I am about to tell you mattered.

I have looked at my life not as a photographer, but with the perspective of a painter rendering a self-portrait. The images that appear here are more as they would appear on a canvas than in a photograph.

This is my personal myth; an allegorical memoir of the adventure of a lifetime. Maybe it will seem familiar to you, too.

SUMMER

It was July 20, 1969, a day of promise. An early morning mist adorned the swaying dune grass. A breeze stirred; a sparrow sang its gentle song; a golden light rose slowly over the ocean.

The sea foam rolled in, along the edge of my fish-shaped isle, and dissolved over my toes as I tried to rub from my eyes the remnants of the night. And I thought, "Each step I take this day promises to soothe the shortcomings of yesterday."

Call

For the first time in my twenty-four years, I had an entire day filled with thought, reflection, and questions. It felt as if a long-dormant part of me was beginning to awaken. Never before had I been so wrapped in meditation.

I was a counselor at a summer camp in Southampton where I had been drawn by the expectation of a meaningful experience. There I became friends with the head counselor, Richard, who had come to the camp for similar reasons. We soon discovered that we had much in common and decided to try to implement a Summerhill-inspired approach to carrying out activities at the camp. We would not steer the campers toward desired results every moment, but instead would encourage and support them so they could learn to make decisions for themselves.

We believed that a democratic approach would contribute to their thriving, and might eventually make them better prepared to assume adult responsibilities. We made it our responsibility to ensure that the campers would have an equal say in how things were run and what activities were planned for them. Richard and I wanted to be there with them, and for them, guiding their efforts at community building. Though the camp director's stated purpose was to challenge and inspire the campers, we were repeatedly thwarted in fulfilling this goal, because his actions were in direct opposition to it.

Richard's every attempt to carry out the camper's reasonable requests were met with increased resistance by the director. We were frustrated, the

3

campers were growing upset and angry, and the experience was growing less camper-centered by the hour.

About midway through the camp session, during a break after dinner that glorious day, I was out walking along the nearby shoreline. It seemed as though something had to—and was about to—give. I began to anticipate what might be next.

I was filled with excitement when the inner voice I had not heard for years spoke:

Awaken and become conscious of that part of yourself that is part of everyone. Allow yourself to pass beyond the gate of limits into a land of wonder where boundaries cease to exist.

Listen every day as if each sound was just for you to understand. Feel the life in each moment as it comes to you.

Immediately I sensed that something more meaningful than I had known before was possible, even imminent.

When I returned to camp, the other counselors and the campers were all gathered around a television set in the dining hall. The feeling in the room was electric, as if something else of consequence was about to happen.

My thoughts still floating above the shoreline, it was a few moments before I could focus on the image I saw on the television screen. Slowly, a broad panorama of a barren landscape took shape. The surface appeared soft and grayish, with small craters scattered about.

The picture faded out, then a light appeared and slowly grew larger. The strange landscape again came into view. This time, a thin metal rod pierced the soft surface. As the camera pulled back, I could see that the rod was the leg of a space module. In a flash, its three other legs appeared.

Then came the first sign of movement. A figure in a bulky suit and thick boots began to climb backward, slowly and cautiously, down a nine-rung ladder. One booted foot touched down, silently displacing a flurry of powdery dust. With the second foot on the surface, the figure then began to move about as if learning to walk.

Soon, a second heavily suited figure joined in. Together they glided about, setting all sorts of equipment in place. Before long, one gave the loose powder a playful kick.

They began to bounce around, hopping across the moon's surface like children of the universe. The words coming from the television set penetrated my mind: "One small step for a man, one giant leap for mankind."

As the camera pulled back and shifted direction, there in the distance was the earthrise, a vision of pure beauty, the entire planet as one—strong, yet fragile. This picture struck me as the most compelling photographic image imaginable.

It was the first time I had really seen the earth without boundaries. It occurred to me that the planet is our sanctuary, and each and every one of us on it makes up its collective conscience. In this vision, with nothing to divide us, the earth appeared as one country. And with billions of individual minds thinking a diversity of thoughts in every corner of this shimmering globe, it became apparent that all of humanity shared a common destiny.

This day *was* different from all others. In seeing our earth from space, I began to see myself differently. How could I find my place within this larger whole? At the same time, I could feel my consciousness shift from the part to the whole, and expand to a breadth I had never before fully considered.

As I sat with our little community, I wondered if anyone else was seeing this the way I was. It was too soon to know, but it seemed like there was a deeper significance to this "giant leap for mankind." Could our new vision of the earth be as much a spiritual leap as a technological leap?

How much more are the possibilities for the future now also expanded? Will this great adventure bring us into a new relationship with one another and our universe? How can we not realize that we are all tied together?

Too many questions for one moment, yet I was infused with a sense of hope that these things would come to pass. Capping a decade of deep change, I could even begin to sense this hope in the reaction of the campers.

When the television was turned off, the campers asked if they could stay up a little later to discuss what they had just seen. Richard and I supported them, and were quickly impressed with their insightful reactions to the significance of what they had just experienced. But no sooner had they begun than the director characteristically put a stop to this endeavor.

It suddenly seemed like our experiment with equality and self-determination with the campers was nearing its end. We felt frustrated and defeated in achieving our goal at the camp, yet satisfied that we had tried our best given our circumstances.

Later that evening, after the campers had all gone to bed, I went out to the dock to reflect further. With my legs dangling, I sat looking at a sea of stars, the reverse perspective of the image we had just seen up close on the television screen. The moon, in its cycles, seemed to reflect the cycle of my own life, maybe even all life, with its ebb and flow, fullness and emptiness, and repetition of these opposites.

Then it really sunk in. The moonwalk removed all barriers for us. Our new view of the world as a whole gave us a different perspective on what was possible after a long decade of changes. At that moment, bits of unedited, still-raw memories from the '60s came pouring back, year by year, through my mind. . . .

1960, my first year of high school, was when everything in the distant world began to seem much closer, as if the world was getting smaller. Television had brought images into our living rooms that changed our views of the world we lived in: rural and urban poverty, global threats of nuclear weapons, and domestic signs of racism, a social disease much worse than we imagined, all became too evident.

I was interested in folk music and doo-wop, but the emergence of a new global sound, a deep drumming tradition from Africa, in a new album called *Drums of Passion* by Baba Olatunji, along with the first black student sit-ins, helped transform a nascent civil rights struggle into a full-fledged national movement.

Raising our hopes even more, the election of John F. Kennedy changed the entire atmosphere of the country—maybe even the world—at the outset of the decade. And his goal of landing a man on the moon before the end of the decade held more promise than we even knew.

1961 saw things go in a different direction, as another wall of separation went up, dividing families and relatives in the city of Berlin. Threats of nuclear weapons led to ban-the-bomb protests worldwide. Home bomb shelters were built. But at the same time, President Kennedy established the Commission on the Status of Women to make recommendations for action toward gender equality.

1962 was marked by nuclear attack threats, frequent civil defense drills, and a stare-down over missiles in Cuba before we realized how close the world had come to nuclear annihilation. And as the pendulum kept swinging, President Kennedy ordered Governor Wallace to admit black students to the University of Alabama, while James Meredith was blocked from attending the University of Mississippi, which lead to tragic riots and senseless deaths.

1963 began with hope and closed in despair, as the women's rights movement took another giant step with Betty Friedan's best-selling *The Feminine Mystique*, which signaled the beginning of the end of the idea that women were less than equal to men, though men have been very slow in understanding this. And at a massive Civil Rights March on Washington, Dr. Martin Luther King Jr. spoke eloquently and powerfully about his dream of a land united across colors and differences.

But then, as I prepared to go home from college for Thanksgiving break that year, life came to a complete halt. President Kennedy was assassinated in Dallas. I had so many questions that were beyond just the loss of one life, even one that had made such a difference in the lives of so many. How could such an unthinkable thing happen? What had we become? How could we ever recover? This loss represented the worst of what we had allowed our society to tolerate. Had a climate of hate and violence, that Malcolm X referred to as becoming a way of life in America, really taken over? What could be done to bring back a balance in this endless battle between progress and regress?

In 1964, President Johnson announced his War on Poverty, and the Civil Rights Act became legislation, outlawing discrimination of any kind. But could a law change behaviors, attitudes, and values that have persisted for so many generations? When three more civil rights workers were killed that summer in Mississippi, the answer was clear. And the war in Vietnam raged on, even with the Tonkin Gulf Resolution.

1965 began with the needless assassination of Malcolm X, who, after his pilgrimage to Mecca, had returned to the U.S. determined to spread a new message: that our problem is "not an American problem, it's a human problem; not a Negro problem, it's a problem of humanity; not a problem of civil rights, but of human rights." He was not given the chance to carry this message any further.

This was my sophomore year in college, and I had decided to major in philosophy to pursue answers to the questions that most intrigued and perplexed me. This gave me glimpses into classic and modern philosophy, and opened up my interests in classic mythology and comparative religion as well. At the same time, civil rights marches continued, antiwar protests escalated, and more race riots ensued.

1966 saw the founding of the National Organization for Women "to bring women into the mainstream of American society now . . . in fully equal partnership with men," seeking to fulfill a 120-year-old vision, as well as more race riots and stronger opposition to the Vietnam war.

1967, a month before my college graduation, saw hundreds of thousands of protesters, including Martin Luther King, demonstrate at the United Nations in New York. I knew that *I* needed a change at this time, too, not only from my campus, but from the East Coast to the West Coast. I applied, got accepted, and was eager to begin my graduate work at the University of Washington.

Right after graduation, I drove out to Seattle and started my studies in a field I thought I wanted to pursue, library science. But after a month of beginning to learn how to catalog books I realized that I really wanted to try my hand at writing them instead. I dropped out at the end of June and took the long route home.

I headed south, through Oregon to California. I was going to San Francisco, having heard Scott McKenzie's song many times. Drawn first to the corners of Haight and Ashbury, I joined in the flow of the throngs of young people gathered around the Panhandle of the Golden Gate Park during the summer of love.

With a renewed sense of expectation, I drove back across the country to New York. But I soon heard all about the race riots in Detroit, Newark, and more than a hundred other cities that summer.

Despite the many distractions, I managed to think a bit about what I was going to do next, and serendipitously came upon an announcement of a new graduate program in American folk culture. I knew immediately I wanted to pursue this, and started the program right away in September. My new studies drew me right in to what they had to offer, but trying to stay focused became difficult.

1968 opened with news of the Tet Offensive, launched by the Vietcong at Nha Trang, and CBS anchor Walter Cronkite calling for negotiations to end the war. By early April, it again felt like hope had been lost, as the illustrious life of the foremost spokesperson of nonviolence for this generation, Martin Luther King Jr., came to a devastating end. The image of his friends and associates on the balcony of the motel pointing to where the shots came from is still fresh in my mind.

Two months later, the assassination of Senator Robert Kennedy cut short his bid to unite a fractured nation. Once again, two more unthought-of events changed everything and caused a book-full of unanswerable questions in my mind. Fittingly, as Senator Kennedy's body was transported by train across America, thousands of people spontaneously appeared along the tracks in towns and cities, all standing in silent tribute.

With so much madness already that year, it was not surprising that the demonstrations against the war turned violent in Chicago and received more attention than the Democratic Convention itself going on there. The year closed with Richard Nixon elected as the next president, by a sliver of a margin of the popular vote, on a platform of "law and order" and the promise that "the long dark night for America is about to end."

My flood of memories brought me back to 1969, which started off with a series of violent campus uprisings spreading from one side of the country to the other. The cover of the April issue of *Rolling Stone*—an image of a bloodied protester, his head on the ground at the mercy of a billy club–wielding policeman, with the title "American Revolution 1969"—mirrored what we were living through.

I knew I would never forget that in May I had lost a childhood and high school friend, Wayne Meyer, to the war in Vietnam. Remembering the times that helped us grow—childhood birthday parties, cub scouts, adventures in the woods, overnights at the cottage on the Sound, boy scouts, our first adventure out of town on our three-speed bikes across the Sound on the ferry and into Connecticut and back, and more—I prayed for his soul, grateful for the memories but deeply saddened for his ultimate sacrifice.

It was difficult, almost painful, to come back into the present after this seemingly endless torrent of ups and downs. I tried to quiet my mind for a moment, to rest from the ongoing rush of all that I had recalled, trying to be still with all that had happened. The war *was* on my mind all the time, but my heart tried to keep me where I was in each moment.

The '60s had been a decade that changed a generation, for better or for worse. One of the things I learned from the moonwalk, and my reflection on the '60s, was simply that the whole is greater than the sum of its parts, that the whole is always the first and foremost consideration. The moonwalk, capping this lurching yet luminous decade coming to a close, was surely a giant leap for humanity; it gave me much hope.

From this perspective, it is as if an old, decaying—perhaps dying—way of being in relationship with one another was ending, while a new way was gradually being born.

I knew I was at the cusp of a great change of my own. But I wondered: What is in store for me? Is my direction known? Can hope truly continue? And I fell asleep that wondrous night quite content.

In the morning, after the campers began their activities, Richard and I had a chance to process what we were experiencing. Through our struggle as advocates for the campers, we had found an affinity of purpose. We each had a sense of what was in the other's thoughts before we spoke.

When he told me he had already decided to leave the camp, I was not surprised. What he had wanted to accomplish was no longer possible here. I was still unsure whether I would stay or not.

"Part of me feels disillusioned, too," I confided, "but another part of me is hopeful." This moment recalled for me the first time I had ever heard my "inner voice" and drew its message right out into the open. I knew I could share my most intimate conviction with Richard, and that he would understand my deeper dilemma. "Since I was a child, I have wanted to know our Creator. I'm sure there is a purpose to life. I must find my role in it."

"Our dreams hold glimpses into the future," he whispered.

"Today, with the moonwalk, we have seen ourselves as never before," I continued. "We have been given a fresh glimpse of reality. Our world has changed right before our eyes. Yet in the next moment, we are right back where we were before. How can we balance these two realities? There is so much more to know."

"Our way of transcending even the subtlest of limits," he said, "is by following our dreams."

"But I feel torn," I told him. "I don't know whether to remain here, go with you, or embark on my own quest."

"Greatest is the dream that awakens those of others. Hold on to yours," he advised.

That exchange connected us like never before. We both knew that I would leave the camp too.

Feeling certain I'd be guided to the right destination, I slept well that evening. In the morning, I knew clearly what my next step should be. I would turn in my resignation and spend a few days with Richard at his parent's summer cottage on nearby Shelter Island. There we would reflect together on what had just happened and on what we could have done differently to enrich the campers' experience.

We took the short ferry ride across the bay and arrived at his cottage, which was situated in a beautiful spot by the water's edge. After a sail around the bay, we plunged into the business at hand: developing a deeper understanding of ourselves, where we had come from, and where we were going.

We decided to approach this task methodically. We would take turns guiding each other on a twenty-four hour inner exploration, free of distractions and other concerns.

We began with Richard as the explorer and me as the guide. I would accompany him wherever he went on this inner journey, supporting him, accepting and validating what he had to say, and encouraging him to continue. Our goal was to become better acquainted with our souls, so we would know where we would be going next.

The first day, which we spent both inside the house and outside on the lawn overlooking the bay, was filled with hard work, some scares, many insights, and new understandings. I both followed and led him where he needed most to go, and it felt more like an eternity than a day.

On the second day, with Richard guiding me to the depths and heights, the shadows and lights, of my being, I explored the mysteries of my life, trying to ascertain their meaning. After a long look at how my parents had influenced me, I realized their love supported me in ways I didn't even know until now. Their love was ever-present, and always felt, but unspoken.

The meaning of my own silence also perplexed me. Through more self-reflection, I understood that I needed to make an extra effort to speak my own mind, to act confidently, and to be more daring. Most important, I would have to work hard to break out of my pattern of silent retreat; I needed to assert myself to create my own destiny. I knew that to become my true self I had to free myself, at least temporarily, from the mold my parents had offered me.

I became poignantly aware that there would always be something within me that I would not be able to fully express, as I was still in the process of becoming whole. And I came to understand that if I surrendered my individual will to the universal will, I might feel a benevolent power aiding me in making the choices I faced, in connecting more deeply with others, and in adopting and holding the right attitudes in each situation. I was determined to place my trust in this larger will.

The insights gained and lessons learned made these two days the most intense and fruitful of my life. In giving our secrets and dreams over to each other, Richard and I shared more of what we really cared about than we even knew was there, and discovered more about ourselves than we had expected. With compassion and non-judgment, we became a friend to each other's soul.

By the second night I was refreshed, and keenly aware that something more was awaiting me. I knew I had to follow my own path, wherever it might lead me. I also knew that I was embarking on a new beginning.

Early the next morning, I left Richard at the cottage on the island, took the ferry, and for a brief interlude wandered along the shoreline at Montauk with the wind at my back.

As though a weight had lifted from my shoulders, I felt hopeful again, eager to taste and touch my future. From observing my life close-up, I knew I could accept whatever might happen, and be content with it.

The sea-spray sparkled, gemlike, animating the world around me. Gulls with spread wings plunged into the bountiful waters and emerged with bits of nourishment. Rocks—some huddled together, some off on their own—stood firm against the onrushing tide. The waves washed ashore, singing of an eternal journey.

The cliffs rising overhead, sighted ships and birds, all the while catching the words of beachcombers. Steadfast, they watched the unveiling of the ever-changing sea beauty; theirs was a vision of universal order.

Again my inner voice spoke:

Let the day go by with no thought of time. What clock can confine eternity? Does the flower growing in the sun check a timepiece every hour?

Time is the matron of evolution; its womb is the moment. Only the living moment reveals the wonder of eternity.

Come, let us go forth together, catching each moment as if it were a lifetime. There never was a moment more real than this one.

The morning sun was high above the sea as I wandered on, deep in thought. Soon I saw a circle of children playing in the sand dunes, lost in the joy of summer. At first I felt separate, alienated from them. What did I have in common with them? How could they be so absorbed in life's simplest pleasures?

Then I remembered that as a child I was not who I am today. I, like these children, had secret places that gave me joy, favorite spots in the woods, or along streams, that allowed me to feel at home. I, too, once had a sense of wonder and a carefree curiosity that pulled me to explore my surroundings.

As an only child, I was accustomed to being by myself, and managed to find plenty to do. I much preferred, however, to be with others.

Drawn to this circle of children, I could see in them something authentic and oddly familiar—an aliveness and wakefulness I had to struggle to maintain. They had not yet lost their innocence. Their joy is the real thing, pure and unsullied. Perhaps I have left childish things behind too soon. I need to let my joy out and rediscover that eager, excited child within me.

So I joined them in a romp across the sandy beach; its softness awakened my toes, and I felt each grain as part of my boundless home. With the waves playing a soothing rhythm upon the shore, everything around me contributed to a natural harmony.

I gazed once more at the children drawing pleasure in the moment. And again my inner voice spoke:

Children, in their purity, are the ones with the open eyes; they see the mysteries clearly. A child's desire is the wind's desire, a mirror of the earth's movement.

Though the leaves are bound by the seasons, they flutter with joy in the summer breeze. Though the trees sleep in winter, they stand with inner certainty of their spring awakening.

Though the nightingale is blanketed by the skies, it soars in its own heaven. Within the ocean, the fish swim freely. What shackles have we, but those we strap onto ourselves?

Our greatest freedom lies in recognizing our connection with all of creation.

Assistance

Leaving my new young friends behind, I was eager to find my own way. Everywhere I went, it seemed that each twig, each leaf, was open to the warm call of life, eager to fulfill its promise, as was I in the summer of my soul.

One morning, a local newspaper headline caught my eye: "Hudson River Sloop Arrives at Port Jeff Today."

I immediately remembered the year before when I had first met Pete Seeger, a friend of Harry Siemsen, the Catskill Mountain folk singer I had interviewed. Pete had given me some background information about Harry, and he also told me that he was raising money to build a replica of an old cargo sloop that had plied the river a century ago.

He and lots of other volunteers would sail her from port to port, teaching people to love their river again. The sloop was called the *Clearwater*, and it was run by the Hudson River Sloop Restoration, which Pete said was probably the first organization to have a bard as chairman of its board.

Recently launched in Maine, the *Clearwater* was on its way to New York City. This was my opportunity to see Pete again, and maybe sail on the sloop. But would he remember me? Would there be room for me? What would I do onboard?

While my mind pondered these uncertainties, my heart knew where it wanted to be. So I headed for Port Jeff. Letting my courageous self take over, I found the sloop at the dock and spoke to Pete.

"Do you remember last year, when we talked about your project and you said I might be able to help? I really would like to. Maybe I could gather stories from people who can tell us what the river was like in the days of the sloops."

"I think you've got something there," the troubadour replied. "The history of the river should be told, too. We could use your help on that. Can you meet us in New York this weekend and sail with us so we can work out the plans?"

"I'd love to!"

I could hardly believe my ears. For three years Pete and his singing friends had given "sloop concerts" up and down the Hudson, raising money to build the *Clearwater* and save the river. His dream had come true, and now *I* was to have a part in it.

The next day, hundreds of people lined New York's South Street Seaport pier in a spectacular expression of support. Under a skyline draped in gray, a fleet of tugs, sail boats, and other launches surrounded the broad-beamed, green-hulled sloop. A single mast held its billowing white canvas aloft, and young seafarers stood proudly upon its deck.

The sloop glided into its berth, as the crowd remained expectantly silent. Within moments Pete Seeger—the banjo-playing, mind-stretching, shelter-giving humanitarian—bearded and wearing a sailor's cap, stepped up on the stage and surged forward in the breeze to share his vision.

"Who's going to clean up this river of ours? No polluter, no politician, is going to lift a finger unless we insist on it. So we have to make ourselves heard. We're all in this environmental thing together. Not even a millionaire can escape it. We've got to take action right now. We may have to start small, but each of us can do something. First, we can all do some reading. Get copies of the books we have here on the ship. Find out the facts about the environmental crisis. Then talk it up."

"The idea is simple," he continued. "We want people to come down to the river again. But the most important thing is to get together. Because we just won't make it unless we can talk to one another and agree on what we have to do. All of us. Young and old, black and white, rich and poor, longhair and crew cut. We hope people will say, 'Gee, this river is a mess. Ought to do something about it.' You see, everything in the world is tied together. You clean up a river, and soon you have to work on cleaning up society. Let's all get together and make this thing work. We can do it. Don't let anyone tell you we can't. But we have to want to do it!"

As he broke into song, "Sailing down my dirty stream, still I love it and I'll keep my dream," I couldn't help but think along with him "that some day, though maybe not this year, the river will once again run clear."

When the music stopped, the people cheered, echoing his enthusiasm. Then the haze that had blurred the skyline slipped silently away.

I knew this was where I belonged. It was evident not only in what he had written around the edge of his banjo skin—"This machine surrounds hate and forces it to surrender"—but in how he embodied love in all that he did.

Later that afternoon, I joined the other seafarers for the sloop's maiden voyage up the Hudson River. I was the newest crew member, and the only non-singing one. The others—"Ramblin'" Jack Elliott, Don McLean, Gordon Bok, Brother Fred Kirkpatrick, Jimmy Collier, Len Chandler, Lou Killen, Andy Wallace, Jon Eberhart, and Captain Alan Aunapu—had all performed on stage with Pete.

We sailed around the tip of Manhattan, passing the Statue of Liberty and entering the mouth of the river in a boat the people of the Hudson Valley hadn't seen in nearly a hundred years. I laid back, taking everything in.

That first day, skyscrapers and factories loomed overpoweringly from the shoreline. Clouds of smog hung over our heads. Conveyor-belt highways were teeming with cars, driven by people who were themselves driven by the demands of time and place.

Our sloop meandered along at a pace set by winds and tides. It took most of the day to reach the George Washington Bridge, at the north end of the bustling island. I thought of the travelers who had made this same voyage to Albany in the days when sloops carried real cargo as well as passengers. They must have seen lush grass and wildflowers growing along the shore, and taken in the sweet smells coming from them.

That night, at anchor in a quiet cove, after a delicious dinner from the *Clearwater* galley, most of us followed Allan, Jack, Lou, and Jimmy into the small hold below the foredeck. There they sat around picking and singing whatever tunes came into their heads. Allan sang some Caribbean songs he had learned while sailing there; Jack let loose with some Woody Guthrie songs he had picked up while traveling with him. For hours we listened to songs, old and new, never wanting the music to stop. And I found that singing is not only a way of earning a living but more importantly a way of life.

The next day, the rock wall of the Palisades, topped with hemlocks, oaks, and tulip tress, towered over our little sloop like a natural fortress, as we plied our course, drifting lazily along in an eternal flow.

But I began to wonder how I would fit into the routine of shipboard life. I felt out of place among seasoned seafarers, a stranger upon unfamiliar waters. They all knew their tasks, their roles. What about mine?

I asked Allan, our captain, who was as much a virtuoso on the ship's halyards as on his guitar strings, "How can I play an equal part in this community?"

Peering over the side of the ship, with his golden locks flowing in the wind, he replied, "Listen to the music of the surrounding waters. The fish silently reveal a secret. They swim as one, sensing the spirit that binds them with their surroundings. With trust and a common will, they carry on as an endless wave in the sea of creation."

At that moment, in the Tappan Zee, the river valley came alive with the call of adventure.

Our every move was determined by a wind charged with power. We took a tack to starboard, and with a mighty slap, back came the mainsail, flapping loosely across the deck. A gust filled the canvas, and as we picked up our course on the port, the lines were pulled taut. Listing in a brisk gale, we headed for a cove, seeking safety as the ship's rail dipped below the sea spray.

At the foot of stern mountains, unseen streams roared down into the river. Amid the sea's ever-breathing energy I, the novice, began to feel more comfortable. I pitched in, hauling a line, and found my place within the seagoing community.

After the squall passed, I climbed out onto the bowsprit and rested in its hammock-like netting. There I regained a perspective on the sea's inner order.

Ahead lay Nyack, our first port of call, where we docked for a sloop festival. By sunset a few visitors were still aboard the sloop. Some were talking with crew members on deck, while others were singing by the tiller as Allan played his guitar.

Sitting on the quarterdeck was a young lady in a wide-brim hat, gazing out over the river. She beckoned me with her soft, silent presence. But without knowing just what I would say, I walked over and greeted her, "Hi. Are you from around here?"

She looked up and smiled. We spoke for a few minutes. I learned her name was Judy and that she was home from college for the summer. We decided to leave the sloop for a walk in the park.

We soon came to a playground and jumped on the swings. After a while, we tried the seesaw, learning little bits about each other with every up-and-down movement of the plank. We walked up a hill, rolled down it, and lay in the warm grass, talking some more.

Later, as we headed back to the sloop, I said, "Hey, you know, this has been a real special night."

"Yeah, it has."

"I sail again tomorrow. We'll be in Albany by next weekend."

"That's the day of the festival," she said excitedly.

"That's right. We'll be doing another sloop festival there, too."

"No, I mean Woodstock!"

"Oh, that one. Are you going?"

"Yeah."

"Well, maybe we could meet there."

"They're expecting thousands of people," she exclaimed. "How would we ever find each other?"

"Easy. We'll meet in front of the stage at noon on Sunday."

"Well, I guess we could try it."

"Great," I said. "Don't forget."

"I won't. Well, I've got to find my little sister and get her home."

"It's been really nice. See you Sunday."

"Yeah. See you at Woodstock."

Threshold

The sloop set sail early Monday morning, tacking through the storied hollow. I sat bare-chested, high upon the crosstree, bobbing to and fro.

The ship revealed to me a secret of the whole unto itself, caught in a purposeful yet unpredictable flow. Moving upon the waters in stately procession, all parts work together as a unit. For each rope that is pulled in, one is loosened.

The sea gives up secrets, too. Forever breathing droplets fall through my fingers, yet hold up the ship that glides upon its surface. The sea sleeps not, yet is endowed with life's eternal energy. I realized it is the magic of this perpetual motion that has lured me away from the land.

Sailing through the highlands, we gazed at the beauty of the river valley at its finest. Gently rolling mountains crowned with forests afforded a delightful contrast between the blue of the river and the sky.

Once in Albany, with the sloop safely moored, and after another local celebration, Allan, an old sailing buddy of David Crosby, two other crew members, and I left late Saturday night for Woodstock, to see for ourselves if this touted event was really about peace and music.

We arrived at Max Yasgur's farm, amidst the rolling fields, just before dawn, during a quiet moment between sets from the night before. The rumored closed highways were all clear, and we found very little movement at all, but were quickly told by those we passed that it was now a free concert.

Everyone was settled in, spread out on the hill around the massive stage area, either sleeping or resting, right where they had been listening to the music all day and night. Those that we found awake welcomed us with friendly faces.

Soon, upon the imposing stage, with towers of scaffolding holding aloft many speakers, we heard "Good morning people. It's a new dawn." And the sounds of Jefferson Airplane came billowing across the sea of awakening souls.

Singing "The Other Side of This Life," these sentiments fit perfectly with mine: "I don't know where I'm going next, I don't know who I'm gonna be . . ." It did seem as if this were the kind of setting where secrets would be shared and where both sides of life might become better known. I managed to find an open spot and sat down to enjoy the music.

A little later, I eased my way toward the seemingly mile-long stage, careful not to step on anyone in the pathless mass, hoping to find my new friend Judy where we had planned to meet. Starting at one side, pressing up against the ten foot high wood-slat fence guarding the stage, I inched along toward the middle, barely able to make it through the throngs of people pushing in. After what seemed like hours, I had made my way nearly to the other side, and there I spotted her coming toward me.

"You made it!" she cried.

"Yeah, this is absolutely incredible!" I replied.

"I know. I've never seen anything like it before."

As we turned and walked off to the side, Joe Cocker, with his bright tie-dyed shirt and spastic gyrations, came across loud and clear. "I get by, with a little help from my friends . . ."

Before we had gotten too far, a torrent of rains came. We headed for her friend's tent to wait out the storm, but never got there. From the stage, came the announcement, "We're all in the same puddle, and we can work it out."

Stuck in the crowds, amid the rain and mud, we found the people especially friendly. Each was looking out for the other, and freely sharing what they had. There really was a sense of "we're all here together, let's make the best of it." It was exactly what a community should be like.

"It's really great being here," Judy announced to me. "This feels different, like the beginning of a whole new way of seeing things. This is going to change everything."

We enjoyed the people and the music for the rest of the day and evening. Our time together at Woodstock felt like weeks, yet passed too quickly.

In the morning, I said, "This has been a lot of fun. It would be nice to see you again."

"Yeah, it has. I've enjoyed being with you. Let's keep in touch. I've got a little time before I have to get back to college."

We exchanged phone numbers, and agreed to see if there was a way we could meet before the summer was over.

As we walked toward the cars, I thought that these three days of peace and music were not in the least a diversion or even an escape from the ever-present pain of Vietnam and all the other senseless killings in our own land, but a reminder that time is always moving forward, and that we all have to be continually seeking our own deeper presence, our own future, and our own meaning.

Reluctantly ready to leave this experience behind us, we could hear a quiet, but screeching, guitar piece that resembled the Star Spangled Banner, coming from Jimi Hendrix.

My companions and I drove back to the sloop.

As we sailed back down river, through waters pierced by the powerful prow, I gazed at the leaves along the shore, sparkling in a backlit brightness, and up at the puffs of clouds passing overhead. Old seamen, sitting on the pier and eager to relive the days of yore, gazed pensively as we glided by.

And the days on the river passed by, too. One day, approaching the Rip Van Winkle Bridge, I took a turn at the tiller. I held it gingerly, not sure of the play in its motion. Soon I found that while holding this toothpick of a timber that guides the broad hull ahead and lofty mast above, I got a charge of energy and was able to keep the lumbering vessel true to her course.

Slipping under the bridge, I thought of old Rip and recognized that I, too, had broken out of a long slumber. It was as if I had just sailed into the realm of being, where I now became conscious of sensations and truths I had not known before. It was like entering another realm of existence, where awareness was heightened and primary, where the everyday things of this world mattered less, and the mysteries and wonders of life—its spiritual significance—mattered most.

This was a new and refreshing feeling; I sensed a clearer recognition of the vision that guided me, and felt a stronger attraction to that force animating me. In fact, something had come alive within me, giving me greater access to the unknown in myself and to the mysteries of reality.

It felt like the beginning of the process of the unfolding of the seed in my soul. And just as with the dim light of the early dawn where the sun's path is sure to ascend upward, I felt confident that this process would continue from this day on.

In this summer of my awakening, I was getting in touch with my life and, after what seemed like a twenty-year sleep, I was feeling fully present. I saw how the moonwalk affirmed my sense that we are all one people on this planet, how Pete Seeger, who reappeared in my life at just the right moment, was a balm to my soul. His concern and caring ways showed me that I mattered, that I fit into the picture, too. His support, encouragement, and guidance gave me much-needed confidence.

Best of all, I began to feel as if I could leave behind the effects of my stuttering. I had begun to emerge out of silence, and to find and follow my own voice, but I knew that my journey to self-expression was just beginning.

Still holding the tiller and keeping the sloop on its path, my inner voice, with which I was becoming more familiar, silently uttered this prayer: *Gracious, ever-surging sea, gather together for me a few of your wisdom pearls, and spray them upon my soul. I shall gladly accept them as seeds of everlasting understanding, tokens from your ocean of infinite meaning.*

As night fell, we dropped anchor in the serenity of a moonlit tide. The creaking in the rigging, the water gently lapping the hull, a fully brightened moon, and passing clouds occasionally dimming its light, all added to the awe of a perfectly ordered evening.

Though the direction of my life was becoming gradually clearer, I knew that I would still have to face long-dormant parts of myself. With that thought and a cool wind coming on, I could do no better than sleep, nestled peacefully in the furled sail, rising and falling with the breathing tide.

FALL

A brisk wind blew upon the Hudson, the tide ran cooler, the leaves began to shiver, the days grew shorter, and billowy clouds filled the sky. With a stream of watery experiences behind me, and the path ahead unknown, I was caught in contemplative abeyance.

Where I was going became secondary to where I had come from. As earth and sky go their separate ways, it was time for me to leave the sea, so I could feel the beating of my heart, and find the peace of my own silence. With no expectations other than to know myself better, I began to look for a quiet place nearby where I could reflect further on my path.

Retreat

It didn't take long to find my desired sojourn. Pete told me about an empty cabin just down the mountainside from his home. He gave me the name of the owner, I called, and, sure enough, it was available. I went right over to look at it.

The small, two-room cabin seemed a perfect home base for carrying out the interviews I had arranged with the people in the river towns we had sailed to. It offered a convenient mid-valley location, and was set back off the road, only a short walk through the woods to the Hudson River.

I moved in that day. I chopped and stacked logs for the fireplace and quickly got the lay of land, which included a stream that ambled down the hillside to the river. Then I began to settle in.

I had cold running water, but no toilet. Behind the cabin was a privy. The kitchen and living room formed one room, with a huge rough-stone fireplace; the bedroom was the only other room.

Before I knew it, I was struck by an acute sense of aloneness. Not being close to anyone special became very real once more. I was forced to face this sensation head-on. That night I had a restless sleep.

In the morning, thoughts of being alone overtook me. Stepping out into the woods, I recalled the many pleasant hours I had played alone as a child. Yet my dream of union with another was still strong. Shedding their leaves around me, the trees offered a response I was not ready for: I have been left alone to discover myself!

I knew I could not let this insight go unattended. I could not let my self slip away again. My job in this world of silence was to find signs of, and connect further with, my teachers and mentors, those around me and those within me.

I realized fully that this time alone was indeed a gift, a time to go deeper into what I already knew, and to uncover what was waiting for me, all around me. I knew I had to settle in to my abode by reconnecting with those who had already inspired me.

I unpacked my carton of well-worn books that made up my essential library and put them on the shelf. The first book I took off the shelf was the poet of Paumanok, Walt Whitman, who had already taught me that his inner world connected him to everyone.

> I celebrate myself,
> And what I assume you shall assume,
> For every atom belonging to me as good belongs to you.

He was full of apparent contradictions: "Clear and sweet is my Soul, and clear and sweet is all that is not my Soul. . . ."

Yet, juxtaposing opposing forces, he illustrated something greater than the parts. He focused not on a temporal, ever-changing realm but one that does not waver, even with the blowing winds of time. He recognized permanency beyond change.

> I believe in you, my Soul—the other I am must not abase itself to you,
> And you must not be abased to the other.

Whitman, the reconciler of opposites, taught me of the wholeness of the creation behind its parts, of the continuity across and between the realms of creation, and gave me the courage to always look past the ambiguity of the moment.

And I call to mankind, Be not curious about God,
For I who am curious about each am not curious about God;
(No array of terms can say how much I am at peace about God, and
about death.)

I hear and behold God in every object, yet I understand God not in
the least, . . .

Do you see, O my brothers and sisters?

It is not chaos or death—it is form and union and plan—it is eternal
life—it is happiness.

Walt Whitman, showing me that there was much more to life than what
we encounter on this earth, seemed to establish a direct link back to that of
William Blake, whose *Poetry and Prose* I took off my shelf.

To see a World in a Grain of Sand
And a Heaven in a Wild Flower,
Hold infinity in the palm of your hand
And Eternity in an hour.

Next I reached for *Memories, Dreams, Reflections,* Carl Jung's autobiographical insights into his "inner experiences."

Like every other being, I am a splinter of the infinite deity. . . .
I am astonished, disappointed, pleased with myself. I am distressed,
depressed, rapturous. I am all these at once. . . . I know only that . . .
I exist on the foundation of something I do not know. In spite of all
uncertainties, I feel a solidity underlying all existence and a continuity
in my mode of being. The world into which we are born is brutal and
cruel, and at the same time of divine beauty.

For Jung, too, there were seeming contradictions and opposing forces, but all led inevitably to a greater whole.

Early the next day, with a mixture of anticipation and trepidation, I ventured further into the woods. Reaching to the ground, I picked up a fallen leaf and blew it into the air. As it flew, I followed. Over stones and thorns I bounded, all the way down to the riverfront, where the leaf landed at my feet. The scenery before me was beautiful and peaceful, except for an occasional train.

Gazing into the clear water, I saw my own face mirrored, with an expression somewhere between joy and sorrow. My heart knew I must remain alone for as long as this took; my mind was prepared for deep reflection.

Questions resurfaced, ongoing quandaries I had not allowed myself to fully explore before, and for which I had no answers: Where am I going? What should I be doing? How will I find meaning in my life? And I realized that the life I had been living was not all mine, not entirely of my choosing.

I wondered further: What am *I* capable of? How can I fulfill *my* potential? What is *calling* me? These dilemmas demanded further reflection, and I vowed to seek the answers for myself, no matter how long it might take.

I knew that this would surely lead me to my own inner truth, which might then help me become a guide to others in their search for truth. I resolved then and there to make these concerns the focus of my every thought.

With this as my goal, what room could be left for fear? Being alone could be my lot at any time, but I would welcome it, rather than attempt to fight it or control it. Living fully in the moment, each moment would show me who I really am, what I am capable of, and where my dreams can take me.

Looking up at the azure sky, I felt the presence of something that linked me to the entire world. Turning my gaze back to the water, I saw my reflection once again. This time with an expression closer to assurance, I knew that I could call upon my own muse for the inspiration I would need.

Indeed, with all the life forms about me also alone, yet firm and assured of their place, I, too, could be content just knowing that I was in touch with the greatest teacher, nature, in all her exquisite forms.

That evening, in the shelter of my retreat, I settled in to once again read Thoreau, who had inspired me to seek the solace of the surrounding woods. If there ever was anyone who knew how to live in the present moment wherever he was, it was the tenant of Walden Pond.

Live each season as it passes; breathe the air, drink the drink, taste the fruit, and resign yourself to the influence of each. . . .

I went to the woods because I wished to live deliberately . . . and see if I could not learn what it had to teach. . . . I wanted to live deep . . . and not, when I came to die, discover that I had not lived. . . .

In proportion as he simplifies his life, the laws of the universe will appear less complex, and solitude will not be solitude, nor poverty poverty, nor weakness weakness.

Since he first gazed into the sky at night, as a child, looking beyond the stars, wanting to see God, Thoreau had been a seeker, every day making some new acquaintance with nature, as Emerson had noted in his eulogy to his neighbor. And I wondered, how could I, similarly, draw more from the universe around me to truly know its inherent harmony, connectedness, and natural balance?

Emerson's own *Self-Reliance*, another longtime staple in my collection of wisdom works, offered some hints:

Accept the place the Divine Providence has found for you. . . . He who would gather immortal palms must not be hindered by the name of goodness, but must explore if it be goodness. . . . Good and bad are but names very readily transferable to that or this. . . . A man is to carry himself in the presence of all opposition as if everything were titular and ephemeral but he. . . . When a man lives with God, his voice shall be as sweet as the murmur of the brook and the rustle of the corn.

Here, all names, even if they appear as opposites, when closely examined, become part of a larger whole that embraces all separation. There is, in

Emerson, a purpose in the clash of opposites, and an underlying sacred order to everything, in which we, whether we realize it or not, fit right in and are an integral part.

Before I called it a night, I wanted to go further back in time, to see if I could find any other threads in this fascinating weaving of holistic thinking. I pulled off my shelf the *I Ching*, the ancient Chinese book of changes, seasoned wisdom depicting the organic processes unfolding in nature, in which both Confucianism and Taoism find their roots.

The many possible combinations of broken and unbroken lines in its sixty-four hexagrams represent the continual change taking place in the physical world, each one with clear counsel for appropriate action to be taken. And then I realized that I could actively participate in this organic process by intervening in my own life to create my own destiny.

Richard Wilhelm's introduction to the *I Ching* added clarity to the role of change, revealing that beyond all the change of this world lies a stillness, a oneness, that changes not. Before change came into this world, there was only the changeless. This primal beginning is represented by the circle, the original oneness, while the changes of this world are represented by the circle divided into the light and the dark, the yin and the yang. Duality came into the world, splitting the primal oneness into an above and a below, a right and a left, a front and back, a world of opposites.

Wilhelm said, "He who has perceived the meaning of change fixes his attention no longer on transitory individual things but on the immutable, eternal law at work in all change." This is the eternal law of the Tao, the principle of the one in the many, or the unity of opposites. Change is but the continuous transformation of the one form into its opposite, as night into day; such is the nature of the universal law that links us all to both the oneness of heaven and the dualities of earth.

Understanding the *I Ching* as nourishment for my soul, without further hesitation, I opened the book randomly to hexagram 61, Chung Fu, or Inner Truth. I read the judgment. The image of the gentle wind above the joyous lake brings good fortune. It furthers one to cross the great stream.

Perseverance

Early the next morning, I awoke with an eagerness to again venture in through the wooded spires and wend my way to the mountainside stream. The night rain had transformed it into a spring of nourishment with an energy all its own. It roared down the hillside, announcing its strength to all creatures in the vicinity.

Drawn to its animating motion, I knelt down to meet the rushing stream, blocked a portion of it with my hand, and drank its crystal waters, an elixir to my thirsty soul. As I swallowed, I gazed around me, then toward the treetops, and newfound beauty spread before me. It was as if every molecule of existence burst alive.

With a sharper, clearer vision, I saw for the first time aspects of the world that had always been in front of me. I felt a renewed love for all of life, and a wonder that, uniting me with the pulse of life, sang a song of sweetness to my awakened body.

When I am open to receiving even the simplest surprises, when I am closest to nature's heartbeat, I am able to come face-to-face with the wisdom of the universe. Nature, in her renewed splendor, continually answers even my unasked questions.

Standing before her in contemplation, I find beauty, mystery, and eternal truth. This is the wonder that shall keep alive my deepest awe. And I felt for the first time that my life was mine, and that this moment could last a lifetime.

Further into the woods, I came to a mighty waterfall pounding its way to a small pond below. Imbued with new courage, I waded into the pond and resolutely approached the majestic falls. I looked up in anticipation of making my ascent.

The chilly, plummeting drops began beating upon my face. As my vision blurred, I turned my thoughts inward. I saw the powerful falls as a myriad of singly falling drops, each one as important as the whole. Only in unity did they exert an influence beyond their individual limits.

A surge within propelled me onward, inch by inch, up the stone wall and into the tower of falling water. I began to pull my way, over the protruding rocks until I reached the top.

Here I understood that only in its entirety does a goal appear overwhelming. Each conscious step we take toward where we want to be turns our volition into action, and our intentional communion with nature into our deepest understanding. The unfolding of nature can clarify the mysteries of our own lives, as our inner workings are a reflection of the same universal law.

The waterfall made it clear to me; if a path to a goal appears too tough, we must go on anyway, as we will eventually overcome the obstacles that seemed insurmountable from a distance, or we will discover a new path to an equally rewarding goal.

Seeing eternity with my next step, I claimed the peace of the surrounding woods as mine. I found the creatures of nature happy with the way life is; we hear no complaints from them. The birds are constantly singing. The leaves are brightest just before their fall; they go gloriously. The bee gathers only honey, the sweet nectar of life. The brook, stumbling over many rocks, keeps on going. The tree, swaying in the wind, stands tall in its place.

Though my path would abound with valleys, I knew the peak of the distant mountain was part of me, too. In a land of hunger, I would feel nourished. In the silence of the morn, I would hear a song. In my soul I knew that like the river flowing in its bed, I would be guided onward.

I waded out of the water, and in a moment of autumn ease, sat beside the swiftly flowing stream. As my mind stilled, I thought of my summer rendezvous with the young lady in the wide-brim hat.

I reflected on what this serendipitous encounter meant to me, and realized its significance was of a promise of what might be, sometime in the future, if my good fortune were to continue.

We had gone our own ways, but I was grateful for what she had reawakened within me, not only the longing for an enduring love, but the recognition that it is an abiding love of the infinite that would make such a love possible. This love is the promise of the soul.

And I reflected further, only through relationships with others, where individual differences emerge each moment, could I truly learn more about my soul. And only in a relationship with another, where circles of interactions expand ever outward, could my soul's promise be fulfilled. Such is the paradox of love. We ascend to the love of the sacred by being better able to recognize that which endures. All relationships go through seasons, but only the most mature experience the renewal of springtime. Love is the bridge between the physical and the spiritual worlds, between the temporal and the eternal.

For the first time, the obvious became clear. Being in love means being loving. Love is care and concern in action. Being loving requires a conscious effort in moving beyond the hurdles that come our way while being in love.

The mystery of love is the great mystery of life. Love's challenge has shown me the value of a love that carries my soul to its loftiest perches. I vowed to seek a sacred love, one founded upon a shared vision, a union of spirits, and service to others. I vowed to continue to dream, to live into a love that knows no boundaries.

Grace

My inner gleanings reminded me of the explorations of the soul I had begun with Richard at the summer cottage. There had been times since then when we had wanted to get together but didn't. So I drove out to see him on Cape Cod, where we quickly caught up on each other's adventures.

He, too, had been delving into dimensions he knew little about and had been finding pieces of his truth in many different places. He had studied with a psychic, lived on a commune, and worked with a clairvoyant. I was as fascinated by his awakenings as he was by mine.

After our visit, I decided to take a walk. Sauntering along the shore where earlier pilgrims had widened their horizons, I came to a spot where heaven and earth converged, where the creative and receptive merged.

In a momentary pause of equilibrium, I gazed into the afternoon sky. The sun was hiding behind a rainbow of myriad-hued clouds. But in an instant, the clouds opened before me, transforming into one pure white luminous light. An embrace of warmth engulfed my entire body. A ray of compassion reached in to fill my heart. I felt the imminence of divinely inspired renewal, as real as my own breath.

Reflecting further, I recognized this as the day that the "voice" had spoken to me of so long ago, when I would come to know God. Yet I also knew that this was part of an ongoing quest in which I would never know the divine essence of the Creator.

Back at Richard's place, I said goodbye again and began the long drive home. That night, I sat by the fire in quiet meditation.

Right away, my mind became very still, listening. Each thought that came and left reminded me that thoughts have lives of their own. Some kept me within the space-time continuum marked by beginnings and endings, while others catapulted me into the timeless realm of eternity. It was up to me to turn toward the light meant to guide me. I needed to identify the thoughts most connected to the source of my being.

Then a beautiful tune, with notes of life giving to life, echoed softly. And the familiar voice of timelessness said:

There is but one song to sing, one song to be heard, one song that harmonizes all other notes now and for all time. That is the song of love. For, the love of all life is the continuum along which we evolve.

Had I not been awake to this moment, such an understanding would have passed me by. But now a new burden arose. Can my deeds match my thoughts and words? Had I done something to be deserving of this gift? I could but walk humbly, fully aware that profundity dwells in the mundane, and that the best way to do something for myself would be to do something for others.

Stepping outside and meandering down the hill, I exulted in the feeling of peace within me, despite the changes taking place around me. Crisp, sorrel-painted leaves began to lose their hold and tumble slowly down, deliberately seeking their roots—a sure sign that the season of color had passed its crowning glory.

That night, with a cool wind coming, the woodpile next to my cabin was depleted noticeably, yet I had much to give thanks for. I listened for the music of the spheres to ring its clarion call and guide my soul.

The next day I drove my red VW Bug into the city for a reunion with Jack Elliott, who was playing at the Gaslight Café. Wearing his cowboy hat and spinning yarns of sailing, he sang with a style that made the cigarette smoke in the small basement club seem as if it were coming from a pile of freshly raked autumn leaves. His finger-picking was precise and punctuated, and his delivery detached yet determined.

Jack had brought along his wife, Martha, their baby, Aiyana, and her friend, Wren. During one number, while walking around the tables singing,

Jack spotted some old friends and urged them to follow him back to the stage. One of them was Len Chandler.

Also in the audience that night was another old friend, who yelled out from the back of the room, "You're getting worse every time I see you."

Jack returned the compliment from the stage, "That was Dave Van Ronk. Every time I sing a song like 'Cocaine,' 'He Was a Friend of Mine,' or some other equally bad tune, I have to give him credit."

After the show, we reminisced about our adventures on the sloop. Jack had a few days off before his next gig on the West Coast, and we decided to get in a couple of days of sailing on the *Clearwater*.

Early the next morning, Jack, Martha, Aiyana, Wren, and Bill, another of Jack's old sailing buddies, all piled into my VW Bug to find the sloop. But first Jack had called his pal Arlo Guthrie at his new farm in the Berkshires to see if he wanted to come sailing with us. Arlo said he was busy waiting for the gas man to come and invited us to come up to his place. We decided to do both: sail during the day and see Arlo later that night.

Off we drove along Canal Street, and up West Side Highway. Soon the fanciful stories that made Jack a singer's singer started flowing. Bill remembered a talk-song that Jack did, a Ustinov thing on the Grand Prix, and asked him if he remembered it.

"Oh yeah," he replied. "You remember that thing? Man, that was in 1962. I was just back from Europe. Bob Dylan was living with me in that house where you brought the stuff in off your boat. Number One Sheridan Square. Did you ever get up there?"

"Sure, I remember that," Bill said.

A little while later, as I downshifted, Jack announced to all passengers: "The sound you have just heard is the normal sound of gearing down. Volkswagen Airlines wants you to be happy. Next time fly Volkswagen."

I thought of one of Jack's favorite pastimes and asked, "How did you get started climbing the rigging of ships?"

"I started doing that in 1949, when I was going to school at the University of Connecticut. I used to hitchhike up to the Mystic Marine Museum where the *Concord* and the *Morgan* are. It was a cold winter day and there were no people in the museum, so I didn't worry about being chased. They have signs up: Do Not Climb the Rigging. Disregarding these, I jumped into the whaler's fo'c's'le, changed into my Superman costume, and then up the ladder I flew. A quick glance over the shoulder, no one coming, I climbed up to the rigging. Mounting the lower shrouds, I climbed, hand over hand, foot over foot—hand on the shrouds, feet on the rattlings. I had been instructed by an old sailor man who said, 'When you climb aloft, sailor laddie, you always hold on to something vertical with your hand, some part of the fixed rigging. . . .'

Jack, true to his name, rambled on for about twenty minutes solid, with an amazing discourse on all the technical aspects of the rigging of ships until he interrupted himself while crossing the Bear Mountain Bridge, "Look at the Hudson River at Bear Mountain," he said. "Have you ever seen this? It's one of the most beautiful rivers in America; Columbia, Snake, Colorado, Missouri."

We crossed more bridges and took every road that went along the river. Finally, as the sun was setting on a day that flew by, we found the *Clearwater* in New Hamburg.

After saying hello to everyone, we sat down to a delectable dinner from the sloop galley. Then we had a decision to make: were we going to sail or see Arlo? We looked at one another with indecision and decided to call Arlo once again to see if he could get away for a sail.

While Allan was talking to Arlo, Jack sang the old mainsail-raising song "Bound for South Australia" to get Arlo in the mood. That didn't work. He still did not want to leave his farm.

After talking it over, we decided that Jack, Martha, Aiyana, and I would head to the Berkshires to see Arlo while Bill and Wren sailed the sloop back to New York.

On the way to Arlo's farm, Jack remarked, "This is the first time we've had a fun trip. All the others were for gigs."

Then he told us of one of his longtime wishes: "Someday I'm gonna build my own ship. David Crosby bought himself a fifty-two foot schooner off the money from 'Mr. Tambourine Man.' He first learned that song off a record by Bobby Dylan. Allan sailed with David Crosby on his schooner. Last time I met David—the only time I've ever spoken to him—he showed me a picture of the schooner he bought. He had a big brown paper envelope with a long list of things to buy: matches, rope, sextants, compass, canvas, sail needles, all the stuff you have to have for a boat."

It was around midnight when we arrived at the farm on October Mountain, under a bright, sparkling moon. Arlo, his wife, Jackie, her sister Juanita, and his friend John, all greeted us warmly. We were also greeted by their dogs, Eli, Nose, Plunkett, Poppy, and Ginny.

It didn't take long for Jack and Arlo to start talking about old times. Jack mentioned that the other night at the Gaslight, a lady asked him to sing "Goodnight, Little Arlo," one of Woody's songs. He said he hadn't sung it in so long that he didn't know if he knew it anymore.

Then Jack said to Arlo, "I'm gonna play you a tune."

Arlo replied, "I'm gonna play with you." And right away, along with John, they got their guitars out and began picking and singing some fine, homespun tunes. That started off a long spontaneous session of swapping songs. I felt as if I were right on stage with three virtuoso pickers who were each having the time of their lives.

As the night slipped into early morning I observed a special quality in our host. He was authentic, easygoing, and very down-to-earth, the sort of person who, as soon as you meet him, you think you've known forever.

During a break in the singing, I said to Arlo, "You seem content with what you are doing."

He answered sincerely, "Once you stop and say, 'Oh, this is it,' you find yourself in a position that's not all that together. Not when the world needs so much. Not when everybody needs so much."

He paused for a moment, then continued, "All of the things people do are as important as the thing I do. As a musician, anyway, I feel that the object of a musician is to evolve music. The object of a bricklayer is to evolve bricklaying. And that's what really happens. I evolve it with where

I'm at. The where-I'm-at-ness is the tool, the means that gets it evolved. But I'm more of a person than a musician. I mean part of me expresses what I am through music, so I have to try to be the best musician I can. I enjoy being what I am. But everybody's got to keep moving. That way, things will happen much more gently."

Satisfied, I went to sleep and didn't wake up until the morning light slipped through the window. After a few sleepy-eyed minutes, I went into the kitchen to find Jackie making pancakes for breakfast.

"It feels real good to be here," I said. "It feels like home."

She stopped stirring the batter for a moment, looked up warmly, and replied, "I'm glad. That's the way it should be."

Then Arlo walked in. "Hi, honey."

"Hi, honey," Jackie returned.

"Morning." he said to me. "How did you sleep?"

"Good morning. Great."

"I have a new song I'd like to sing for you," said Arlo.

He placed a paper with handwritten lyrics on the kitchen table, sat down, and started to sing.

Woke up this morning with my head in my hand.
Come on, children, come on.
The snow was falling all over the land
Come on, children, come on

I don't know, but I been told
Come on, children, come on.
That the streets of heaven have all been sold.
Come on, children, come on.

Come on, children, all come home.
Jesus gonna make you well.
Come on, people, now it's time to go
Go to where a man can dwell.

Just then, the overcast sky broke, and a bright ray of sunlight came from behind the clouds, through the window, and right onto the paper he was singing from. Jackie and I looked at each other in amazement as he continued to sing.

Come on, Gabriel, blow that thing
Come on, children, come on
All God's children got to dance and sing
Come on, children, come on

Come on, Gabriel, blow that thing.
Come on, children, come on
All God's children got to dance and sing.
Come on, children, come on

All God's children got to sing and shout,
Come on, children, come on
Ain't nobody round bound to kick you out.
Come on, children, come on

Come on, everybody, what's it worth
Come on, children, come on
To make a heaven out of this earth?
Come on, children, come on

When he concluded, Jackie said, "Honey, that is beautiful."

"It sure is," I added. "And that was quite a confirmation."

"That happened when I wrote the song, too," Arlo declared.

After breakfast we went outside, where the dogs chased anything they could find all over the place and the cats sniffed the fresh air as it blew by. Chickens and goats roamed the yard, ducks swam in the pond, and beyond a nearby stream were green meadows, gently sloping hills, and rugged mountains. We took in the beauty of the landscape as Arlo told us his plans for this newly acquired 250-acre farm.

The chore of the day was to harvest the rocks from the soon-to-be-completed, newly landscaped lawn. We all pitched in, placing the rocks along the edge and building a stone wall fence, while Abe, the Guthries' six-month-old son, watched from his highchair on the porch.

That afternoon Arlo showed us around his land. We made our way along a trail to the top of a gently sloping mountainside. We looked out onto a beautiful valley. To get an even better view, Jack scurried up a pine tree as if he were going aloft on a boat. Arlo and I followed, twisting ourselves around as we climbed, one with the trees.

I reveled in the gift I had been given by this unique individual who had been so open and generous with me. I knew that the land he had taken in trust was in good hands, that the people he would come in contact with would be equally well served.

After dinner, we all sat on the living room floor. Jack played with Aiyana, and Arlo crawled around with Abe, while the dogs rolled around in the middle of it all. Then Jack spotted Arlo's "kid" saddle on a saw horse, and before we knew it, he had thrown it over his back. Arlo helped him tighten the cinches. Then Aiyana climbed onto the saddle and they cantered around the room.

Jack said, "Now I know what a saddled horse feels like. It's not so bad at all."

I imagined Arlo's childhood in Brooklyn, when Woody must have been doing the same things with *him*. Then I remembered a comment Arlo had made earlier that day: "I don't tend to think of myself as his son, but I do think of him as my father. I'm from there, but not originating from there. I believe that children choose their parents. In order for humankind to continue, one of the things that is absolutely necessary is that we surround ourselves with people who help us evolve to the fullest extent possible, and who help create the circumstances that put us in the position to do the most we can in a lifetime. A lot of people have helped me get to this place. If Woody can dig it, that's fine. I'm sure he can."

I, too, was sure Woody would understand where Arlo was and where he was going. I felt privileged to have this time with Arlo and his family, and to have shared with him that sign of acceptance, of confirmation, that had pierced our spirits. I knew that that moment when the sky opened would stay with me, resting deep in my heart, for a long time to come. The story-teller extraordinaire had given me a story to remember, a story to live by.

It was with great reluctance that Jack, Martha, Aiyana, and I left October Mountain the following morning. On the drive back to the city, Martha remarked, "I wish our trip East could have been a little longer."

"We could zigzag," Jack said.

Such is the path of living deliberately, I reflected.

WINTER

Back at my cabin by the river, the days grew shorter as the sun's path drew closer to the horizon. Every day the ice on the stream thickened, as little waterbeds coalesced into a delicately sculptured frieze.

Soft white flakes, each a separate universe, tumbled through the air in unison, weaving a robe of repose upon the land. Soon even the trees fell asleep.

Purification

My visit to the Berkshires had inspired me to explore how symbols, myth, and meaning might further enhance my own life. Reflecting on the warm greeting I, a stranger, had received there, the authentic, earthy quality of my hosts, the experience of the sun coming out and shining on Arlo's sheet of song lyrics, and how these linked to my own background in folklore, I knew I had to learn more about how and why the timeless motifs and archetypes that guided the mythic figures of the past came into our lives, as well.

Where do archetypes come from? How and why are they repeated over and over? How and why did the first archetypal experience itself come about? What do the thousands of motifs and archetypes found in the world's sacred literature really mean to us today? Can they be considered universal occurrences? These being the questions of the season, and this a good time to pursue them, I drove down to the city.

That evening, while looking in store windows along 8th Street in Greenwich Village, a book on mythology caught my eye. I went inside the bookshop, quickly found the volume, and began to page through it. Immediately I was engrossed in a captivating theme: the one story that all stories share, the one pattern that all quests follow.

The book, *The Hero with a Thousand Faces,* described the timeless motifs underlying myths of all cultures. Something about this book was familiar, even comforting. Perhaps it was the message that one archetypal pattern bridged past and present, East and West. I knew I wanted to find out more.

Looking up, I noticed a poster announcing a talk on the themes common to all mythologies—and it was being given by Joseph Campbell—the author of the book I was reading! The talk was scheduled for that evening at Cooper Union, only a few blocks away. Glancing at the clock, I saw that I had just enough time to get there.

Without hesitation, I quickly purchased the book, and walked over to Cooper Union. I sat down in one of the front rows of The Great Hall and reflected on the passages I had just read about the thousand variations on the one pattern, unaware that the thousand seats around me were filling up.

Soon Joseph Campbell was introduced. He spoke brilliantly, with poise and eloquence, never referring to notes. It felt as if I were the only other person in the room and his words were meant just for me: "The universal formula of the mythological journey is separation, initiation, and return: a hero ventures forth from the world of common day into a region of supernatural wonder; fabulous forces are there encountered and a decisive victory is won; the hero comes back from this mysterious adventure with the power to bestow boons on his fellow men. That is the pattern of the myth, and that is the pattern of the fantasies of the psyche."

What I heard soothed my soul. As he went on, everything he said spoke directly to the experiences I was beginning to become aware of in my own life. Each image he offered was pregnant with a meaning I could feel.

He continued: "All my life, as a student of mythologies, I have been working with the universal archetypes, and I can tell you, they *do* exist and are the same all over the world. The myths and rites will be given different interpretations, different rational applications, different social customs to validate and enforce. And yet the archetypal, essential forms and ideas are the same—often stunningly so. The psychologist who has best described them is Carl G. Jung, who terms them 'archetypes of the collective unconscious,' pertaining to those structures of the psyche that are not the products of merely individual experience but are common to all mankind. . . . The inward journeys of the mythological hero, the shaman, the mystic, and the schizophrenic are in principle the same; and when the return occurs, it is experienced as a rebirth. The new ego lives in accord with society and nature, in harmony, and at peace. The ultimate aim of the quest, if one is to return, must be neither release nor ecstasy for oneself, but the wisdom and power to serve others."

The moments flew by as I took it all in. He spoke a simple, straightforward truth. It confirmed my unexpressed feeling that I was already living parts of the mythic pattern. It *was* comforting to know that such truths arise in the same way for everyone, awakening the same awe and revealing the same mystery.

I reflected on the crossroads I had faced in the bookstore. My choices were: stay where I was, move on to something else, or attend the talk right then. In spontaneously following the instinct that tugged at my heart, in deciding to go hear Joseph Campbell in that moment, I found a sacred realm in the midst of commonplace reality. I became more aware of the power of motifs and archetypes, and the meaning and order that they bring to our lives.

The seemingly scattered parts of our lives come together as pieces of some universal puzzle through the organizing message of myth. Our own personal stories, and the revelations that emerge from the soul, mirror that same truth. In the gift of this understanding, I had found my guide, my teacher, the one to help me recognize the sacred pattern in my own life.

At the end of the talk, I remained seated as most of the crowd disappeared from the hall. A small group of lingering well-wishers had gathered around Campbell at the podium. I knew, because of the way his talk had spoken directly to me and my experience that I, too, wanted to say something to him.

I waited a few more minutes to let the crowd thin and to allow my courage to expand. Then I walked up just as the last person was leaving his side.

I cautiously introduced myself, and began what I hoped would come out as I wanted, "What you said really meant a great deal to me. In the images you used, and in the pattern you described, I can begin to recognize my own joys and sorrows. I had never imagined that my experiences have been shared by so many others of different times and settings. There must be something very powerful in archetypal images. I feel like I'm in the middle of that pattern right now in my own life. My experiences confirm everything you were saying. I have been helped along too, just as you described in myth, when I needed it most."

"It sounds like you *have* entered the archetypal landscape," Campbell responded. "You should think about how your experience can be shaped and given form that will make it more than just yours."

"I have a lot more to learn about this pattern, and how it fits into my life and that of others," I said. "Would it be possible to talk with you more about this sometime?"

"Why, sure," he replied sincerely. He wrote down his address and telephone number, handed me the paper, and said, "Give me a call. We can talk further."

I could tell he was serious, and I was surprised by his openness and his willingness to accommodate me. Was there something in me that he sensed needed encouragement? Did he respond like this to everyone who showed a sincere interest in his passion? On the drive back to the cabin that night, I had much to think about. I wondered where his invitation might lead.

For days afterward, the wailing of the winter wind reminded me of the story of my soul. The wind ripped through the trees, which, though appearing bare, empty, and lonely, were actually staunch in their withdrawal for a season of inner growth. Their leaves, each with its special destiny, had long since found the warm comfort of their source. I, too, yearned for such shelter.

The owner of the cabin had warned me that when winter came I would have to find another place to live. There was no heat in the cabin, and the fireplace was unsafe for regular use. I had to bid my familiar abode farewell and look elsewhere for a dwelling place.

I remembered what a friend had told me about a Franciscan monastery nearby. He thought they took in people who needed a place to stay, primarily the homeless and indigent. It felt like a bad joke at first, but the more I thought about it, the more it seemed like a viable option. Although I didn't qualify as the typical guest, I decided to try it out.

As I arrived at the friary, a silent chill pervaded a gray, more than unusually somber, evening sky. A full moon appeared from behind the clouds, giving a fresh sparkle to the night. Along the winding roadway leading up the mountainside to the inn, the bare arms of the trees were raised in a soliloquy of reverence. The faint silhouette of a solitary friar graced the chapel yard.

Seeking only a bed for the night, I was greeted by a warm embrace of peaceful hospitality. The friar in charge, however, had to ask me the standard questions: Do you have any booze on you? When was the last time you had a drink? How long have you been on the road?

I replied, "I had some orange juice this morning, just before I moved out of my place." I must have answered his questions satisfactorily, as he wrote that my condition upon arrival was "sober" and assigned me to bunk 39. It was about midnight when he showed me into the large, dark, warm dormitory room. All the men there were asleep. I, too, fell quickly asleep.

The next thing I heard was bells—the six o'clock wake-up call. I opened my eyes to a new experience: the bond of mutual caring that emerged from the camaraderie of the men in need. Each man had his own reason for seeking out this shelter. Some were addicts, some could help themselves, others could hardly get out of bed unaided—all were without a home. No one had to be told when another needed a hand. They sensed it naturally; they knew it from their own experience.

Each assured the other and was of service in some unique way, if simply to show their gratitude for all that had been offered to them. From amid the helpless arose the saintly as the ailing aided the lame.

One older man helped a younger one dress for breakfast, and he returned a gentle, grateful look as best he could. It became evident that within the comfort of unselfish assistance, sanctity could be found and life sustained.

Having been raised in the Protestant faith, I had never imagined myself in a Catholic monastery. When I was in high school, my two closest friends and I used to spend a lot of time talking about religion. One of them was Jewish, and the other Catholic. Our conversations usually ended up with my Jewish friend and I finding some inconsistency in the Catholic religion. But now I could find out for myself what I had thought I knew about this mysterious faith.

Shortly before, I had begun a comparative exploration of other religions, and found a core of spiritual truths common to them all. As a result, religious matters that had previously bothered me no longer seemed important. My hope was to live by the ageless verities of all religions. Here at the friary, I had my opportunity to learn firsthand the truths of a religion I had all but dismissed.

After we all had breakfast, the friars called up the new men—or at least those who could manage it—for their work assignments. Following chores, I asked if I could go see Father Jeremiah, the guardian father of the monastery. The friar said I could.

I walked further up the holy mountain to the cloistered abbey containing Father Jeremiah's office. He greeted me warmly. His office struck me on the one hand as highly unusual for the spiritual leader of the community, yet on the other as most appropriate. The walls were decorated with colorful contemporary posters and banners. One of them read, "Let happiness and peace reign among us all forever."

I explained that I was in between places to live, working on a research project for the sloop restoration. "I was drawn to this sacred fortress in search of understanding," I added.

With grace in his eyes, the guardian father replied, "You are welcome to stay here. In the friary is an empty cell. It shall be yours for as long as you need it."

I was startled by his immediate, unconditional acceptance of me. "Really? I don't know how long I might need a place to stay."

He answered, "Our door is open to you. We give freely that you may find what you seek. In that way, do we all rise to wholeness."

And so I was given refuge in the old friary, with a cell to myself. Nestled within a sacred womb, I was free to explore the mysteries of another venerable community. The halls of the monastery buildings were open to me. This was my chance to die to the world, to dwell in an inner sanctuary that nourishes the soul.

With access to the friary, the abbey, the chapel, the shrines, the library, the meeting rooms, the offices, and the large dining room where I could eat with all the brothers, I knew I would be able to explore each of the questions that had already begun filling my mind. That first night in my bare cell, I slept with a sense of freshness, comfort, and anticipation.

Awaking the next morning, I felt another part of me come to life. I swung my legs over the side of the bed and wrote as never before. Thoughts flowed out of me in verse, as drops in a waterfall, and spilled into my journal:

With our eyes open to the way,
The wonders of the day
Whisper in our ears,
No time for fears.
Seeking joy, playing my part,
I know in my heart
That eternity is ours,
Though we find thorns among flowers.
To each alone, the day unfolds
What the mystery holds.
No more sadness, no more sorrow,
We have seen the light of tomorrow.

It must have been through grace that I felt the heartbeat common to all, and began to sense the greater meaning of community. I wrote some more, then left my cell to wander through the friary where all things became new before my eyes.

Outside, past dormant gardens, I observed the brothers at their chores, each with a material as well as spiritual role. The gardener, the baker, the mechanic, and the office worker each served their community in practical ways, while also giving counsel and guidance to the visiting laity who came to confide in their word.

That afternoon, I spoke in earnest with Brother Joe, my new brown-robed friend. "What is the meaning of the three knots in the rope belt you wear?" I asked.

"The three knots are for our three vows," I was told. "Poverty, chastity, and obedience."

"They sound like great sacrifices," I noted.

"Our vows draw us toward a higher law. That is where true freedom lies," he assured me.

Through celibacy, could the friar who loves each equally know the love that is most sublime? Could one person's poverty be another's freedom from desire? Could poverty be peace of mind? Could chastity be purity of spirit and, obedience, union with a higher truth?

The following day, my questions focused on the martyr of a thousand ages I saw hanging upon his cross everywhere I wandered. Peering directly into his eyes, I felt his pain in my body; it tore at my soul, as well. How could this be? What is this pain I am feeling? If he is the Son of God, why would he let himself endure such a fate?

This time I confided in Brother Joachim. "Why do we make him look like an albatross?"

"He sacrificed the seed of his life so the tree of his truth might grow," he assured me.

Reaching deep into his heart, he continued, "His sacrifice is the greatest gift of love we have known. No greater love can we comprehend. No greater life can we hope to follow."

After a reflective pause, Brother Joachim added, "There can be no imitation; but since each life has its own burden and its own reward, this love is nearer to you than your own breath."

As I returned to my cell, it sunk in. The love I sought was always within me. But what about hate? Was that always within me, as well? Did I contain *everything* within me? Must I replace animosity with compassion? Letting go of such negativity and unburdened by hate or anger, I could be as water flowing over a rock.

One chilly morning the following week, I took a walk outside the friary and found an iron water tower rising two hundred feet above the mountaintop. Without thinking, I climbed the tower, one thin iron step at a time. At its top, I walked around the platform encircling the water-tower, and gazed out at the natural beauty and majesty of the Hudson Valley and surrounding mountains.

Amid these thoughts of beauty, I looked down at the land and buildings below, and was struck by the possibility of falling to my death. Would I slip? Could I conceivably jump?

Immediately, I understood that my death would have to be accidental. Never would I want to take away my life when there was so much here yet to see and do.

I grasped the cold iron structure more tightly. I was concerned now not so much about death, but about not living fully. When death did come, I knew I wouldn't lose what lasts; I might even gain a great deal more. I only wanted to be able to give the most to each day of the life that I have.

Then another question surfaced: Can I be of any consequence? Up here, not to anyone, but down on the living earth to everyone with whom I can share my truth, was my reply.

I climbed slowly down the steps, and as soon as I touched the earth, I was elated. I headed for the stonewall that circled the friary, sat on its cold surface, and felt an energy warming me from inside.

Then my inner voice returned and spoke clearly: *One yet to know love is as a flower yet to bloom. Let the mysteries of love lead you on.*

Somewhere is a love everlasting and unconditional. Such a love sees with the inner eye, and feels with a heart of compassion.

Love's ascent is steep and treacherous. Expect nothing of love except what you give, for love grows not through supremacy but through equality. The servant of this love recognizes in the beloved a sign of the Divine. At its summit, love becomes the intermingling of two souls.

Divine love is the reason for all existence. Not for a moment does it neglect even one life. Love is a circle, and everyone is within its embrace.

As divine love remains constant, so does love's tenderness follow love's patience. Boundless love—a reality for all to know—takes flight from within the open heart, the heart that knows the love of God. Those who see with the eyes of this heart see nothing but love itself.

Back in my cell, I began in earnest my practice of daily prayer and meditation.

Continuity

The weeks passed. One evening as I walked through the monastery halls, a heavenly sound caught my attention. The ethereal music grew fuller, elevating my soul with each step I took toward it.

I was soon in the doorway of the chapel where, from the golden pipes of the organ, a celestial melody swelled, graced by a chorus of chanting friars. I stood transfixed, frozen in time, as the soothing serenade continued. After what seemed like a few hours, I sat in an empty seat in the rear pew and was soon lost in deep meditation as the chanting went on. My mind contemplated the organ music, while my soul soared in other realms.

Returning to my cell, I got ready for bed, and read from one of my newest books, *The Masks of God: Creative Mythology*. I meditated on the words Joseph Campbell had written upon completing this four-volume enterprise:

> I find that its main result for me has been its confirmation of a thought I have long and faithfully entertained: of the unity of the race of man, not only in its biology but also in its spiritual history, which has everywhere unfolded in the manner of a single symphony, with its themes announced, developed, amplified and turned about, distorted, reasserted, and, today, in a grand *fortissimo* of all sections sounding together, irresistibly advancing to some kind of climax, out of which the next great movement will emerge. And I can see no reason why anyone should suppose that in the future the same motifs already

heard will not be sounding still—in new relationships indeed, but ever the same motifs.

I then looked out the window, and my gaze fixed upon a moonlit bare-branched tree with icicle twigs, standing stiff in frozen soil, looming lifeless. Soon afterward, I went to sleep and fell into a dream . . .

My friend Richard and I are walking along a path beside a river in a thickly overgrown forest. We round a bend, whereupon I stop to look at the variety of vegetation. Richard continues along the trail.

Farther upriver, he comes upon a beaver building a dam. Just then, a wolf approaches. To protect the beaver, Richard leans over with a stick, attempting to force the beaver underwater, but Richard falls into the river and he is carried away by the rushing tide.

Sensing that something is wrong, I run on ahead. Finding no sign of Richard on my side of the river, I look across the rushing tide; everything on the opposite side is still and quiet.

Then I lean over to look in the water, when all of a sudden I, too, am pulled into the river, leaving my body behind.

Like a bird whose cage door has been thrown wide open, my spirit takes flight and begins to soar in a limitless sea of light. The water turns to sky. My senses are heightened; my feelings of happiness, more acute.

Then the voice I had become familiar with speaks with conviction:

The horizon of eternity is right before our eyes, for this is a life without end. Think of the leaves that fall and those that follow in the spring, and be assured, life is everlasting.

What is death but life transformed, a passing from one season to the next, for life follows life. And the life that is to come will surely fulfill the life you have known.

Let not the death of those you love pull you closer to your grave. As their energy merges with yours, the life that is theirs becomes a part of you; thus is life carried on into eternity.

When the spirit is freed from the body, its journey is ever-advancing, toward the great reunion. Its progress is dependent upon the grace of God and the prayers of those left behind. Through the love that is passed on continually, all life evolves.

Comfort overcomes me as the light grows brilliant. I want to know its source but, dazed by its splendor, I turn away.

Then I land softly on a verdant meadow. And a great silence falls upon the land. Again I look toward the light.

This time I see seven angels in the distance, each one standing on a stair step ascending a majestic mountain. I sense that Richard is with one of them.

I approach the first angel, who emerges out of the brilliant light, standing upon holy ground, and he invites me toward him.

"I am searching for my friend," I say. "Is he here?"

The angel replies, "I represent an eternal force, having one common womb, mind, and spirit. I bring knowledge of the One Thing out of which all things have sprung. I speak of one law, founded upon wisdom, justice, and equity. Never shall you be left alone. As I am needed, I am born from age to age."

The gate before me opens, the angel vanishes, and I enter, finding a peaceful garden-land where songbirds raise heavenly melodies. But before long, life falls silent. All that had been green is now withered and barren.

After wandering through this wilderness, I eventually see the second angel, bearing in his hand a sparkling staff, and another door to the unknown swings open.

Drawing closer, I see glimpses of an intriguing land beyond.

I speak to the angel. "Have you seen my friend? Is he here?"

"As the voice of one angel is hushed in the land, another arises to guide your way. In the beginning, everything was good, yet the path to goodness is strewn with many temptations. Follow this path with purity, help others along this path, and you shall surely attain your goal. This is our promise, our everlasting covenant."

The second gate opens, the angel vanishes, and I am ushered into a land of justice and truth. After a while, however, the inhabitants of this land forget the words of the angel and become defiled and aimless. Simultaneously, the landscape turns dark and arid. But again a light shines from the mountaintop to guide my path.

The third angel then appears, bowing with hands together. I approach and say, "I don't understand. I am only looking for my friend, and instead I find words of wisdom."

The angel replies, "Happy is the one who enters, by way of restraint, giving, and undivided love, the abodes of the soul. Revere the earth, make sacred your work, and value all of the peoples of humanity. We are the birthless, the death-less. Common be our intention, perfect is our unity."

Then the angel steps aside, and the gate to another realm opens. Before me lies a land of promise, where songs of praise abound. Yet in time, the people follow their own ways, and as earlier, the spirit of life is lost.

Continuing on my quest, I see the fourth angel, a perfect mirror of light, carrying three baskets. Here I sense a new element to my nature. I realize I had not only been hearing what the angels were saying but attempting to incorporate their words into my spirit.

"In my search for my friend, I am finding my own inner harmony. Why is that?" I ask.

The angel answers, "As you have seen, I am not the first like myself, nor shall I be the last. We are called the enlightened ones. We have each provided a portion of the guidance you need to progress in your journey. Be patient, as you tread the middle path you shall become a lamp unto others, leading the way to universal fellowship."

The gate of this land opens wide, and as the angel vanishes, I walk into a noble, resplendent realm, where truth reigns supreme. But before long, the light dims and all forms of life wither and pale.

A star falls from the sky, and the fifth angel appears, who heralds a vibrant domain. A breeze of contentment blows over me. This time I am silent for want of fitting words.

The angel speaks saying, "Love all who come your way, even as yourself, and great shall be your reward. Walk in the light; let not your heart be troubled. Much more is there to say, but now is not the time. I will return to you again."

The gate to this land opens, and I step into a borderless city teeming with happiness. Yet before long, veils of misunderstanding divide the people and they lose their joy.

Soon the sixth angel emerges from a barren, rocky desert, with peace upon his brow.

"I have noticed a common thread running through the words of the angels," I say.

The angel assures me, "We appear in time of need to confirm the pillars of tradition. No difference do we make between any of us. We are each light upon light. Guided is the one who is submissive. Indeed, you are already on your journey back from where you have come."

Then he ushers me into the precincts of a holy region replete with fragrant gardens of delight beside shimmering streams. Again the people begin to interpret for themselves and fall into discord. I move on, certain I would find the seventh angel.

Hearing a refreshing chant coming from what I think is a heavenly abode, I am drawn instead to a dark, deplorable prison cell. Here many who sought an everlasting truth huddle together about one with a radiant countenance. Though mired in filth and weighed down with chains, they beam with light and joy, and beckon me to join them.

I hesitate, but then realize that this must be the abode of the seventh angel. I step in and am warmly welcomed.

An expectant hush falls over the cell. The angel, holding an open book, says, "This is an ancient, universal, and ever-unfolding faith that we all herald. We clear the path of impediments to your progress. Each angel is from the one source, as rays of one light. Every time one of us appears, it is to build anew the whole world."

The voice of the seventh angel resounds with clarity, and I feel the quickening breeze of life pour over me like a mighty torrent. I take in every syllable as he continues. "A spiritual springtime has arrived. This is the day of promise. This is the time for a world-embracing vision. Dedicate yourself to the service of the entire human family and to the advancement of civilization."

Serenity swells up within me, as the gentle tones of the angel's voice gives me the courage to commit to carrying out my responsibility.

The cell transforms into a mountainside of aromatic gardens, with beds of flowers and rows of cypress trees. A murmuring stream flows beside them fringed with willows; the air, fragrant with scents of jasmine and orange; and in the distance, even the desert blooms. Below, a harbor sparkles with the shimmering lights of ships bearing pilgrims from all over the globe.

Upon the mountainside surrounding me are majestic shrines. Circling them are people from every corner of the globe, and of every hue, raising songs of joy. From all sides of the mountain, melodious voices sound their praise at daybreak.

Renewal

As I awoke the following morning, I opened my eyes slowly, for I sensed a different world around me. At first I could not recognize my monastic cell, nor did I remember going to sleep there the night before.

The bitter cold of the morning, however, snapped me back to reality. Tiny ice crystals on the window blocked my view of the grounds outside, but resting my arms upon the sill and taking a closer look, I could see a layer of frost covering the field below. Off to the right was the same bare-branched tree I'd seen the night before, erect in the frozen soil.

The barren tree brought me back to my dream, which was still clear in my mind. But what was the meaning of the seven angels? What was my dream really trying to tell me?

As I reflected further, I was drawn to the book by my bedside, *The Bible of the World,* which contained in one volume the profound and beautiful scriptural essence of all religious traditions.

I opened the book to a page where a scholar was quoted as saying: "There is but one religion for humanity; the many faiths and creeds are all streams or streamlets of this great river. . . . The Sun of Truth is one. His rays stream forth into the minds and hearts of men."

Could it be that the Messengers of the one Creator reveal this Truth little by little, over time? Then, in this same volume, from the Book of Isaiah, I found, "And thou shalt be called by a new name, which the mouth of the Lord shall name."

And the words of Krishna, in the Bhagavad Gita, made even more sense: "Whenever dharma declines and the purpose of life is forgotten, I manifest myself on earth. I am born in every age to protect the good . . ."

And, from the Dhammapada, I read, "I am not the first Buddha who came upon earth, nor shall I be the last. In due time another Buddha will arise in the world." This, I realized, is exactly what my dream was telling me.

Similarly, in the Gospels, Christ offered this perspective: "I have many things to tell you, but ye cannot bear them now. . . . When the Spirit of Truth is come, he will guide you unto all truth."

And in the Qur'án, Muhammad looked ahead to the "day unto which mankind shall be gathered together" as "a time appointed," adding "To each age its Book." It appeared to me that this sequence of interconnected sacred traditions implied not only the oneness of Divinity but also one evolving knowledge system meant to shed light on Its mysteries.

Then I reached for another well-used book from my shelf, *The Religions of Man,* in which Huston Smith addressed the question foremost on my mind: how, then, do these religions relate to one another? Instead of offering a clear answer, he suggested three possibilities: either, a) one of the religions is superior to the others, or, b) with only incidental differences, the religions are basically alike with towering truths on which they unite, or, c) like a stained glass window, all religions refract the same sunlight in different shapes and colors, which allows for their differences but doesn't impact their relative worth.

To me, it seemed like c) offered a clarification of b), both representing the very definition of religion itself, as he then suggests, "Seeing ourselves as belonging to the whole is what religion—*religio*, rebinding—*is*. It is mankind's fundamental thrust at unity."

This captured my attention, and was where my imagination was taking me. It seemed that there were myriad paths leading from a single sacred origin, that there was a timeless thread connecting each of the paths, that each path led back to the same source—that therefore an underlying unity connected all of the divinely inspired traditions. I realized that I had a responsibility to focus my own search for truth on such wholeness.

As I thought more about these sacred traditions, each one having a founder entrusted with a special message, I remembered a brochure I had picked up at one of the sloop festivals during the summer that described divine revelation as relative, progressive, and unfolding across time.

I went to find this brochure, which was tucked away in one of my books for safe keeping until the time was right to reflect upon it. The brochure explained how each of the founders of the world's religions came from one Source and are the rays of one Light, their teachings differing one from another only because of the varying circumstances of the time and place in which they were released. Throughout history, these spiritual energies have had the purpose of guiding humanity's spiritual progress toward the fulfillment of its promised destiny.

In essence, the brochure was saying that we are living in a spiritual spring-time, with a new spiritual epoch having been initiated by the revelation of Bahá'u'lláh in the mid-nineteenth century, which is designed to awaken humanity to a new way of seeing the world and our relationships in it. Ultimately, as its seasons continue to unfold, the future we all want will be ushered in as we utilize the spiritual tools it has provided to get us there.

This was beginning to sound like the understanding I had been coming to through my own search. The brochure went on to list the core teachings of Bahá'u'lláh, founder of the Bahá'í Faith, as re-visioning *religion as one evolutionary process*, and recognizing *humanity as one family*. Supporting these primary principles were others that would also be required to bring all of them into being, such as: *the independent investigation of reality; the equality of women and men; the elimination of prejudice of all kinds; the harmony of science and religion; the elimination of the extremes of wealth and poverty; universal education for girls and boys; and, a universal auxiliary language.*

And I thought how could we ever have *peace on earth* without consciously putting these interconnected spiritual principles into action first?

I couldn't help but reflect on this, and found it remarkable that the Bahá'í Faith emerged with a worldview built upon the oneness of humanity in the mid-1800s. There was no getting around it; these were the most needed principles for resolving the most challenging issues of our time; implementing them might be the only way we would overcome the greatest threats to our collective wellbeing.

It seemed to me that the Bahá'í Faith offered a beacon of hope, and a vision of unity, while ringing a clarion call to action, as these words of Bahá'u'lláh indicate: "So powerful is the light of unity that it can illuminate the whole earth."

I recognized that a process begun millennia ago is today reaching a critical juncture. Humanity stands at a spiritual and social crossroads, and it is clearer than ever that only our own individual commitment—and action—will enable this process to move onward toward the culmination we can only vaguely imagine today.

It occurred to me that seeing the world's religions not as separate, independent, competing entities but rather as a single tree consisting of ever-growing, complementary branches may be a matter of our own survival.

As I looked into this further, it became evident that from this one tree had flourished the Indigenous traditions branches, the Abrahamic branches, and the Dharmic branches, or all the world's sacred and spiritual traditions. And it seemed pretty clear that if one universal law governed the entire creation that this same law would govern the evolution of religion.

This holistic perspective also offered a way of envisioning religion as we do science; though both have their many branches, and both are unfolding, evolving knowledge systems revealing the truths of the same ultimate reality, at the deepest level, religion is religion, as science is science.

And then the idea of a spiritual springtime brought to mind more of what actually happens in each natural cycle. There always seems to occur a struggle to move beyond the decay of winter, a slowness to let go of the old, before the new finally comes into full bloom. We have seen plenty of this during the twentieth century already, with global conflicts and wars, but the stronger effort to bring into being universal human rights has made progress undeniable in recognizing that, though it expresses many differences, humanity *is* one family.

Even with struggle, it still appears that the peoples of the world are more alike than not, have more to say to each other, and more to learn from each other about our common spiritual heritage and our destiny. Could it be that our greatest gift to one another is simply to listen deeply, with open hearts, to the stories of faith we each carry?

All this reminded me of, and confirmed, Joseph Campbell's statement upon completing his four-volume set, *The Masks of God*, that there is a biological and spiritual unity to the human race. It also caused me to wonder if Carl Jung might have been envisioning this convergence of East and West when he said in *Modern Man in Search of a Soul*, another essential work on my bookshelf, that "we are only at the threshold of a new spiritual epoch," since "imponderable psychic forces" are transforming human life.

I turned my gaze out the window, and saw the cold pallor of the winter land-scape transform in full-blown animation. The roots of the dormant tree stirred beneath the hardened soil, pushing a new life force up into its frozen limbs. Fresh buds appeared, leaves unfurled, and the boughs turned verdant again.

I then felt a new life force growing within *me*. Odd as it seemed, the presence of my grandmother became so strong that I sensed she wanted to tell me something important. Could it be that she had been with me every step of the way? Was she helping me make sense of the unknown? Just as she silently guided me in life, maybe she continues to guide me even now. Life and death could be one indivisible reality, between which consciousness can flow as freely as the wind, I thought.

Once more I heard the voice I had come to believe in:

As you face your challenges in life, remember to be loving, gentle, and respect-ful in every circumstance; remember that life is a recurring cycle of crises and triumphs, both necessary parts of the whole. Love is the mystery that unites opposites, transforming sorrow into joy. I will be with you always. Yet you are your own guide, too. You have been a good listener; now listen to the truth of others, for in listening well you give your love.

As I looked up again, the tree became the center of a bountiful garden, transporting me back to the paradise of my dream. And I thought that maybe it had been with my grandmother's help that I had made my way through the dreamscape, too.

My task became even clearer: to live lovingly, and greet all that comes my way with grateful appreciation. With this as my focus, I would be able to offer a steady hand in the circle of humanity.

As the days passed, my thoughts at the monastery came relentlessly back to the promise of the vision that had sprung to life that bitter morning. But how, exactly, would my task be carried out in the world? What role would I slip into that is meant just for me in this world? I became all the more ready to find it.

Finally, one Sunday, I could wait no longer within the cloistered walls of the monastery. The ice and the snow had long since melted. The brook beside the abbey swelled as it rushed by. Daffodils brightened the fields, and the sun was higher than it had been for months.

I made my way through the long narrow halls to the guardian father's inner chamber. I paused a moment, and then knocked.

I was ushered inside, and with gratitude for the guardian father and the friars seated there, I explained: "I found my way to your sanctuary from another tradition. I had no intention to wear the robe, or take on the vows. I wanted only to live more deeply, and see if I could experience a spiritual life. Yet you gave me shelter and more. You even referred to me as the 'unfrocked friar.' This is indeed a blessed spot, and I found more here than I could have imagined. I have uncovered the roots of my destiny. I am grateful to have shared your home. Now I must reenter the mainstream of life."

The guardian father, moved by my heartfelt affirmation, stood and approached me, extending his arms. After embracing me in a spirit of brotherhood, he whispered in my ear, "Spread your joy around the world."

Brother Joe and the others wished me well, too. The next morning, I loaded my meager belongings into my red VW and drove down the holy mountain.

SPRING

Nature was shaking off its long rest. Songbirds struck up a symphony. Newly arrived flower buds dotted the bare twigs of the tulip trees. Wild berries began to claim their color. Raindrops lingered on pine needles.

The Hudson itself was vibrant with runoff from the mountains. Everywhere, the fragrance of seedtime announced a season of fresh growth. And a gentle breeze nudged my soul.

Return

I drove toward New York City without knowing exactly where I would end up. As I thought about my options, it seemed like a perfect time to visit Joseph Campbell, if he was available. I called him; he remembered me and was able to see me at four o'clock.

I arrived at his home in Greenwich Village, and he greeted me as warmly as he had the first time we met. He invited me up, introduced me to his wife, Jean, and showed me into the den, where we sat down and talked. I told him, in more detail, how my adventures seemed to have led me from one archetypal opportunity to another.

"That is similar to my own adventure when I was 'on the road' around your age," he said.

We spoke for what seemed like hours about how life mirrors myth. His enthusiasm and vitality were beyond any I had experienced, as was his understanding of life's sacred themes.

As our time together came to a close, he said to me, "The archetypes in your experience represent your most reliable truth. Integrate them into your everyday living. Transmit their meaning to others."

I expressed my deep gratitude to him for sharing his insights with me, for showing such regard for my life and its possibilities, and for the practical knowledge his lifelong study of mythology had brought me and so many others.

On my way to the car I remembered, solitude has its season, but the decree of spring is fellowship. I got in my car and headed eastward, eager to see my old friends and tell them of all that had happened to me.

Once on the expressway, new questions arose: Who, having seen a boundless world, would return to the old? The world I had called "home" was as different from the one I now know as heaven is from earth—Who would believe what I had seen? Who would understand what I had to say?

Torn between two realities, I recalled Richard's words just before we left the summer camp: "Greatest is the dream that awakens those of others."

Right away, the power of my own vision returned, as strong as it had been when I first felt it in my heart. I realized more fully that the realm of mysterious wonder is but a deeper layer of everyday reality.

I understood that we are not only free to pass back and forth between the two realities but *must* do so, in order to plant seeds of understanding in the garden of the spirit. For in reality the two are one. It was then that the parting words of Joseph Campbell took on even deeper significance.

Without further delay I continued on, desiring first to return to the familiar shore, lined with fresh dune grass, and immerse my toes in the soft sands of the isle of my birth. The moment I saw the sparkling waves and darted in and out of their sea-spray, pearls of assurance washed upon me, bringing joy to my heart. The feeling of being home again was greatly welcomed.

The next morning, I stopped by my alma mater, the college with its windmill on the hill. While walking through the hallway of the new humanities building, I came upon one of my favorite professors.

"I *thought* that was you," he said. "What have you been up to?"

I explained all that I had been doing, and he brought me up to date on the changes that had taken place in the three years since I had graduated.

He went on to say, "This is good timing. We're offering a course this term called 'Contemporary Folk-Rock Lyrics as Poetry,' but the instructor just decided to spend the time working on his dissertation instead."

"Really? That's a topic I've become very interested in," I said. "I've recently found many timeless themes in today's folk-rock lyrics."

"Maybe you could help us out. Would you consider teaching the course?"

"Oh, I'd love to!" I said instinctively, without fully knowing what I would encounter.

Later that day, after my appointment was made official, I had second thoughts. I wasn't sure I was ready to take on this opportunity. It would be my first teaching experience. Would I have enough time to prepare? Would I know what to say? Would I be able to say what I wanted to?

In the end, I had to admit that although being a teacher would challenge the image I had of myself, it could fulfill my desire to assist others in reaching their potential. Maybe it would even help *me* leave my childhood silence behind.

I settled into my decision and went right to work fleshing out the syllabus, getting the lyrics together, and thinking about the context within which I wanted to present them.

We would trace the development of the music and culture that had become known as folk-rock; we would consider representative lyrics for their aesthetic appeal, their philosophical value, and their historical and contemporary meaning; and we would discuss, from a mythological perspective, the themes that emerged. Some of the songwriters to be studied would be Bob Dylan, Arlo Guthrie, Joni Mitchell, James Taylor, Carol King, Paul Simon, Cat Stevens, and Laura Nyro.

But I also knew I needed to explore much more what teaching and learning meant to me, and how I could best facilitate that vital process.

First, I remembered Plato's allegory of the cave, in which the shadows on the wall were the cave dweller's only reality. But as soon as a cave dweller steps outside, a new reality appears, and the shadows are recognized for what they are—illusions. It may be that everyone brings their own cave with them into the classroom. I thought, if I could help guide my students beyond what is familiar to them, into the openness of a new, previously invisible expanse, I might be able to add light to their lives. In applying my study of philosophy, I wanted the practice of inner reflection to be a regular part of the course.

Emerson again came to my mind. His talk at Cambridge on the American scholar offered me much at this moment. He knew nature was first in importance of the influences on the scholar and how this impacts the overall purpose of "higher" education: "Colleges . . . can only highly serve us when they aim not to drill, but to create; when they gather from far every ray of various genius to their hospitable halls, and, by the concentrated fires, set the hearts of their youth on flame." In Emerson's musings, I had found a great challenge as a new teacher.

Then I thought of A. N. Whitehead's *The Aims of Education*, in which, after starting out from a math and science perspective, he then says, "the essence of education is that it be religious." By this he means an education that develops a sense of "duty and reverence," or an understanding that we can "control the course of events," and also that "the present holds within itself the complete sum of existence . . . the wholeness of time, which is eternity." And I realized if I give the greatest value to the timeless, the universal, and the eternal, that I would be approaching the essence of education.

Then I remembered *Black Elk Speaks*, and wondered if a classroom experience could come anywhere close to recreating the mystery of being in the heart of nature *and* hearing a voice meant just for oneself, as he had heard: "Behold a sacred voice is calling you; all over the sky a sacred voice is calling." I thought this kind of experience could be like hearing one's inner voice, the voice that lifts one to the heights of understanding. This kind of holistic learning could help my students see more than they could tell and understand more than they saw.

It was clear to me that my emerging philosophy of teaching and learning reflected who I was; it came directly from my own life experience, and from the influences that had had the greatest impact on me. This was what I knew best.

I wanted most to engage my students in a process of shared reflection, so we could learn from each other what our deepest motivations, convictions, and questions are. If this collaborative effort worked well, we would become a community learning as much from ourselves and each other as from any textbook. And in so doing, we might tap into the reservoir of the spirit.

My hope was that I could convey what I had discovered to others, create a setting within which a reflective approach could have relevance for others, and inspire their own creative thinking.

By the time the class was to start, I felt as ready as I could be to take on my newest challenge.

Gratitude

On the first day of class, we sat in a circle and I looked into the faces of my students, one by one.

I spoke freely and truthfully; words poured forth, as if flowing from my soul: "My job, as teacher, is to help you uncover the wisdom already within you. Your job, as learner, is to be open to your own mysteries. My challenge is to facilitate this process; yours is to seek the meaning that makes the whole greater than any of its parts.

"What is learning if not uncovering the secrets buried within? Are we not learning every second we are conscious of the lives we are living? Our greatest wisdom comes from the vast expanse within us. Everything we learn reveals the beginning of something more to be learned. Your own experience—and the understanding you gain from that—is the source of your greatest learning.

"Like the gardener who carefully prunes his plants, I would remove what is in your way. I would guide you beyond the surface of your mind, and past the walls of your daily routine, to the deeper meaning of your life.

"Something within us all lies untapped until we let go of whatever we think we need to hold on to. Our detachment from the material world lifts us into a greater awareness of life's boundlessness, timelessness, and sacredness. In this realm, we bring into being the realization of our own potential.

"Open your eyes to the moment, grasp the wonder of its existence. Everything, big and small, is a clue, each important in its own way. As the morning glory's moment of brightness can be an eternity, so can a moment of quiet deliberation serve you for a lifetime.

"The universe is our classroom. Everything we need to know is unfolding all around us. Within the workings of nature are revealed divine lessons with each passing season. Let your curiosity lead you further and further into life's mysteries. The education that matters the most, and prepares us for a life of learning, is that which connects us with our own spirit."

I took a deep breath as I looked around at the students again. They had been listening intently. We went on to introduce ourselves, and then to an overview of the course and syllabus.

As that first class came to a close, I realized that I could trust myself, that I could speak for myself, that others would listen to what I said, and that, for the first time, I had been speaking with my inner voice; I wanted only to be able to call upon it whenever I needed it. I imagined it as the voice of love, my greatest ally.

Beginning with the next class, as we engaged in discussions of the meaning of many contemporary folk-rock lyrics, especially how the songs follow the mythological journey of separation, initiation, and return, the students and I became better acquainted. A couple of them remembered me from when I was a student at the college.

The first song we listened to, a song expressing the archetype of separation, was Arlo Guthrie's "Highway in the Wind." I passed out the lyrics so we could follow the words along with the song.

Sail with me into the unknown void
That has no end,
Swept along the open road
That don't seem to begin.
Come with me and love me, Babe,
I may be back again.
Meantime I'll keep sailing down
This highway in the wind . . .

The fortune-teller tells me
I have somewhere to go.
I look and try to understand
And wonder how she knows.
So I must be going now,
I'm losing time my friend,
Looking for a rainbow
Down this highway in the wind.

The first response from a student was, "When you really listen to the words, the song sounds even better. It makes even more sense. But is it poetry?"

I tossed the question back to them, "What do you think? Looking at the song lyric as bare lines of words, with nowhere to hide on the printed page, is a tough test for any songwriter to pass. What *does* make a lyric a poem?"

One student said, "It rhymes, it has verses, and it seems to have meter."

"It expresses experiences, feelings, and emotions," said another.

"It seems different than regular speech. It seems to carry more power, too."

"And, it uses words, images, and ideas that many people can relate to, and maybe even understand from their own experience," noted another student.

"Very good," I commented. "Sometimes a song can say strikingly sensitive and penetrating things that most everyday conversation can't even touch. There are images, metaphors, and meanings in Arlo's song that do seem to stay with you. It may be that one of poetry's greatest contributions is to be able to pass timeless meaning across very different times. Arlo seems to be echoing the experience and sentiment of Walt Whitman, who wrote:

Afoot and lighthearted I take to the open road,
Healthy, free the world before me,
The long brown path before me leading wherever I choose.

Henceforth I ask not good-fortune—I myself am good-fortune.

"And Whitman may be echoing William Blake, who was echoing Dante, who in turn echoed Homer. Times change, but life's most important issues remain constant."

Then we listened to a few more songs on this theme, Joni Mitchell's "Urge for Going," James Taylor's "Country Road," Cat Stevens's "Father and Son," and others.

The students quickly became adept at recognizing the timeless motifs in the songs. One asked, "How can there be so many different experiences and situations to express the same theme?"

I tried to explain, "We're just beginning to look at songs that mirror a timeless pattern. Identifying the elements of this pattern will become even clearer as we go on. These songwriters are speaking from their own experience, and their sentiments are real. But they speak of life as it has always been, and always will be. Their poetry represents not only our age, but also the archetypal experiences played out for millennia.

"What we have heard so far represents the first phase of the mythological journey, the archetype of the 'call to adventure,' when we leave the familiar behind and enter a new realm. As Joseph Campbell says, experiencing this archetype 'signifies that destiny has summoned the hero and transferred his spiritual center of gravity from within the pale of society to a zone unknown.' There are many ways this 'fateful region' can be represented, in every corner of the world, but all are expressions of an independent search through which we find our own truth."

In the next class, we listened to songs of initiation. First in this group was Laura Nyro's "Time and Love."

So winter froze the river
And winter birds don't sing
Winter makes you shiver
So time is gonna bring you spring

He swears he'll never marry
Says that cuddles are a curse

Just tell him plain
You're on the next train

If love don't get there first
Time and love, everybody, time and love
Nothing cures like time and love

So Jesus was an angel
And mankind broke His wing
But Jesus gave His lifeline
So sacred bells could sing

Now a woman is a fighter
Gathered white or African
A woman is a woman, inside
Has riches for her man

Time and love
Nothing cures like time and love.

The first student responding said, "This makes it clear that we always face challenges. But it is hopeful, too, in that we can overcome them in time."

Another said, "It also seems to say that giving in to temptations can be a real challenge. But if we just wait a moment the next thing may be better for us."

And a very perceptive student pointed out, "This song is very relevant to our time because it brings in the contributions of women; they are at least equal to those of men. And not only that, it values all people in the same way."

"What I like," said another, "is how it's not only time that heals, but love, too."

"You have all made important points here," I added. "Life is an ongoing initiation, and each situation we find ourselves in is really meant to assist our progress. Most of the challenges we face are inner struggles. There *is* built-in hope in the mythological journey of the hero, but we need something to guide us through the challenges and temptations, like a clear standard or set of personal values.

"Joseph Campbell said that 'woman, in the language of mythology, represents the totality of what can be known.' Maybe women's rights, along with civil rights, have finally found their time to be fully understood and brought into being. Related to this is that the boon itself to be gained from the arduous mythological journey is a love that is boundless. This realization goes a long way in bringing about the renewal and rebirth central to the journey."

We went on in another class to consider the lyrics of songs of return. Here we listened to the Moody Blues' "The Balance."

After he had journeyed,
And his feet were sore,
And he was tired,
He came upon an orange grove
And he rested
And he lay in the cool,
And while he rested, he took to himself an orange and tasted it,
And it was good.
And he felt the earth to his spine,
And he asked, and he saw the tree above him, and the stars,
And the veins in the leaf,
And the light, and the balance.
And he saw magnificent perfection,
Whereon he thought of himself in balance,
And he knew he was.

Just open your eyes,
And realize, the way it's always been. . . .

And he thought of those he angered,
For he was not a violent man . . . ,
And he understood. . . .
And he learned compassion.

And with his eye of compassion
He saw his enemies like unto himself,
And he learned love.
Then, he was answered.

We pondered the printed lyrics a moment more. "This kind of understanding seems like it would take a lot of work," one student offered. "When the journey is completed it's not really over, it requires deep, thoughtful reflection."

"And probably many questions, too, about what it all means," said another.

"Sometimes, momentarily, I might be able to see 'magnificent perfection,' in nature, especially, but to be able to see this in myself, or to see myself in balance, that seems like quite a stretch," another student revealed.

A student added, "I wonder if balance on the personal level leads to balance on the social level. This song may even be saying something about balance between social and economic extremes, too."

"I can see this song having implications beyond the personal, too," another said. "The '60s *were* a time of extremes, with the pendulum swinging from one side to the other so often and so quickly. All we could have asked for was a balance between the two."

"Yes, I think that's it," said another. "It was all so turbulent and chaotic, too much, too fast. If it had all happened slower, we might have felt the balance more."

"It seems to follow, if more people find this inner balance, it would add to the balance in society," another commented.

"I can relate to the difficulty of seeing this balance in myself, not to mention society," said another student.

And another added, "This balance the song speaks of is really some kind of middle ground between heaven and earth, very difficult to find, much less maintain."

"I think you are all identifying the reality of this part of the journey very well," I said. "It is not easy for the adventurer to return with a gift that is understood or readily received by others. This may be the greatest challenge of the journey that never ends. If, and when, we come to this understanding, what do we do with what we have been given?

"First is to accept the responsibility that comes with the understanding. But our survival at this point depends upon the realization that the two kingdoms are actually one—different parts of the same whole, and that if we live consciously with the understanding we have been given, if our gift is given without expectation, and if we accept whatever our place in the world is, we will be able to move freely back and forth between the two realms, and be grateful for our life."

Then I added, "Even, or maybe especially, during a time when a war in a far away country demands much of our thoughts, as these songwriters have shown us, we still have our own lives to live. We still have to figure out what they mean for us."

After considering a few more lyrics in this vein, like Cat Stevens's "On the Road to Find Out," Bob Dylan's "New Morning," and James Taylor's "Lo and Behold," our heartfelt discussions had brought us together as mentors to each other, learning together from the themes and issues in the songs. And the course became like a workshop where everyone expressed what was foremost on their minds.

In the next to last class, while in our circle, a student took the entire course to its most practical level, asking sincerely, "What we have talked about here has been stimulating, but what can we *do* with it? How can we *use* it?"

I replied, "When you find a song, a poem, or anything else, which speaks directly to you, you have found the essence of your own life, an answer to one of your own unasked questions. Find something in the journey of another similar to that of your own, and you will realize you are living the journey of the soul.

"The timeless truth of myth is being carried out each day of our lives. These songwriters express a current mythology in the language of today, created from real experiences of chaos and despair, love and beauty. This new mythology relates not to a wilting past, but to a planet of conquered horizons.

"Each one of us has experiences that connect us to others. This is the usefulness, the lesson, within the archetypes of myth. As we respond to their living truth with belief and lasting commitment, we are introduced to our universal self, the hero or heroine of our own adventure. And it is this understanding that may become the most practical of all learning, as we carry out our lives in conscious relationship to others."

I paused for a moment, wanting to see if they were still with me. It seemed like they wanted to hear more, so I went on, speaking from my own experience. "You have a choice in all your actions. The decisions you make determine your destiny. Each day as you strive to bring forth your inner virtues, your inner goodness, your own divinity will emerge. The greatest need in the world today is for each of us to know intimately our own spiritual nature, to live into our spiritual calling."

Then a student who had not yet spoken stopped me and said, "Spiritual seems to be one of those words that can have many meanings. What do you mean by that?"

"Yes, this is a term, like many, shrouded in mystery, but spirituality has a long history in this country, and beyond. The Transcendentalists understood spirituality as our deepest interior cravings, what we all aspire to; as the poetry of the soul, expressed with an energy that connects us to the divine; as a contemplative stillness, allowing a freedom of insight; as a religion of the spirit.

"Yet living a spiritual life is totally subjective. It is doing what matters most to you, it is being aware of what you most passionately love, it is carrying out a deep respect for the mysteries of life; it is doing what is personally sacred to you. It is knowing what draws you to and connects you with all of life.

"As you come to know your sacred self, a longing will grow within you, all separation will vanish, and you will find yourself deeply connected with all life around you. Your true calling is to valiant acts of service. All your endeavors can be as a prayer, if carried out with the intent to increase the visibility of love in the world."

And another student asked, "But how can we know our true calling when those closest to us have other plans in store for us?"

This question had flowed as naturally as what had preceded it, and I knew this was the opportunity everything in the course had been leading up to. "Before it is too late," I answered, "get to know those who have given you life. This will help you discover your own uniqueness. It is out of your parents' union that you have come forth to find the union within your own self. If you follow your own heartbeat, you will encounter the hurdles meant to ultimately propel you to your own fulfillment.

"By adhering to your own internal integrity, whatever work you do can become worship. The work most fulfilling is that which contributes to justice among the peoples of the world; the work most comforting brings one soul into communion with another.

"When you are in touch with your true nature, you are able to know gratitude for all the gifts received, even those not wanted. Gratefulness comes with giving up control of what is beyond your control. Regardless of what you have been given, your greatest gift to those who have given you life may be forgiveness for what they were unable to give you.

"As the tide returns to the shore, so do we, each in our own time, return with greater love for the source of our being. In this way, you become a blossom of their spirit. You may even find your greatest reward someday in the children of *your* spirit."

"You were a student here just a short time ago," said one who had known me before. "How have you arrived at such understandings?"

I felt I needed to respond to this honest query by explaining even more fully my own experience. "It is not always, or even necessarily, the passage of time, or age, that brings such understandings, but, even more so, our own deep reflection on the experiences we do have. I have been to places that seemed to be waiting for me to arrive. I have come full circle, returning to where I began my journey, yet nothing appears quite the same as it did before.

"My own understandings of the experiences I have had have added depth to my soul, only because I became aware of what was happening to me as it happened. I took time to let each experience sink deep within me and become a vital part of me. I looked for hidden dimensions in the clear-cut. My experiences became most useful to me when I was able to recognize how they connect me to everyone else.

"When I discovered that the mythic pattern was what I was living, through reading what I was most deeply drawn to, and through being guided by a mentor who had discerned this pattern in his own life and in the lives of the classic heroes and heroines, I saw with different eyes.

"Now I see the whole before the parts, the universal before the particular, and the perennial before the changing. Might this understanding be available to us all, as we seek to recognize the underlying spiritual laws of the universe?

"It seems that every generation has found this in their own way. Emerson, with his idea of the one soul that links us all, along with Thoreau and Whitman, spoke with this consciousness in the last century. Before them, the purpose of all the great prophets of all the great sacred traditions has been to explain what is beyond our physical world, and what the patterns are that uphold this transcendent reality. Joseph Campbell, Carl Jung, and others speak of the universal spiritual realm today.

"In our own generation, many of the songwriters we have listened to seem to express this understanding. We are the first generation to see our wholeness reflected back to us from the moon. It is our challenge now to have what is not readily visible to a quick glance, become, through deep reflection, the obvious.

"The meaning I have found upon my path is very personal, yet at the same time something you may know directly. Perhaps my experience is a mirror of yours yet to come, an echo of what you already know within your heart.

"Could it be that our dreams parallel one another, and converge as we pass on to others the gift we have been given? The myths and adventures of previous ages come to life through living our own lives fully and deliberately. Our lives, too, become mythic as we experience the universal, timeless truths in our own way.

"To stumble once in awhile is part of our journey. Taking that first step into the unknown enables us to find our greatest support, to learn that we are not alone, and that others before us have also walked our path. Every place you have been, every thought, worry, and fear you have ever had, is already part of our collective experience.

"Confronting the unknown with courage reveals to us a capacity greater than we thought we had. Facing difficulty gives us greater confidence; experiencing success gives us a glimpse of what is to come. Even temptations contribute to our growth when we hold firmly to the values we have set for ourselves.

"Sooner or later, along our path, a deeper responsibility begins to stir within us, awakening a new desire to discover how fulfilling life can really be. This is your moment to arise, to give back the love you have been given."

After class, surprised by my own voice, I was confident that I could be honest with myself and also speak my truth to others. Through this experience, I have come to better understand my role in the teaching and learning process.

And I was beginning to feel as though maybe I had found my direction, even my calling. I knew from my own experience now that I could welcome each moment as it came, and be grateful for what it brought.

Vision

In the final minutes of the last class, after having become comfortable with each other and our deepest thoughts, I wanted to speak as clearly and openly as I could. "Early in my youth, I enjoyed many quiet walks on the beach beside these waters. Here, my inner purpose took root, and grew within me.

"Dreams have a pulse of their own and seek their own attainment. In your heart is a vision waiting to come forth and guide you. It will unfold in its own time, slowly transforming your life into a miracle.

"We each walk a sacred path every day of our lives. Its holiness becomes clearer with each conscious step we take. Listen carefully to the silence of your own heart, and you will hear the sacred voice within you.

"We live in a time of engagement, not withdrawal. Fellowship and harmony are the brightest lights of a life well lived. Follow your own dream to a better world."

A student who rarely spoke asked, "How can you see a world filled with hope when we see despair all around us?"

At that moment, I was reminded what a privilege it was to be a teacher, to facilitate such an exchange of sincerity. I answered firmly, "The despair you see is real, yet it hides a world that is visible only when you look with the eyes of love and oneness. Hope and despair coexist, and fuel each other always.

"All things in this physical realm change in time. The pain we see around us does not last forever. A dark night is but a brush stroke from the morning light. Even the journey of the soul has obstacles in its path. Be patient, everything that happens is all part of a sacred pattern of change and renewal.

"This pattern of birth, death, and rebirth is designed to bring about transformation, yet sometimes people get lost in the middle—or muddle—of the process, see nothing else, mistake this for their destiny, and feel stuck there. But time refuses to stand still and urges us on to complete the process.

"There are forces assisting us each step of the way. A sure sign that we are moving closer to our goal is when we sense that we are in a hopeless predicament, but at the last moment, some form of aid or guidance comes from an unexpected place, giving us the means to carry on, and it is then that we find a resolution to our muddle.

"The personal and the collective despair we see around us is transitory yet purposeful, like the muddles that come and go in our lives. They will take their course, here one moment and gone the next. Both happiness and sadness have their places in this world. But we needn't get caught up in either."

Another student asked, "Is this 'collective despair' the kind of thing McLuhan was warning us about with his idea of the 'global village'"?

"Great question!" I responded, "The global village we recognize more and more that we do live in certainly does have the potential to become a place where despair takes over. But our growing interdependence also has the potential to bring us socially, culturally, and even politically and spiritually closer together, too, as a world community. The technology turning the world into a village is but a neutral tool; we who use it can give it meaning and maybe a morality.

"The potential of this inherent tension has been with us forever. It was Socrates who said, twenty-five centuries ago, 'I am not an Athenian or a Greek but a citizen of the world.' Never has there been a time when this inclusive identity was more vital, or more possible, than this very moment. The world grows smaller with each day, with each thought of the whole. This deeper, fuller identity represents our greatest potential.

"The key to the direction we decide to go is already within us. Like a ray of light from the sun, our soul gives us our only changeless identity, the one which we are endowed with at conception, and which we carry with us throughout eternity.

"The soul identifies us as divine in essence, and is what affords us the spiritual progress we make in this world. The soul's inclination is always toward the loftiest realm. It is guided solely by the power of love, which is the primary cause of the betterment of the world.

"Though we carry many other identities, we have but one essential identity that remains constant throughout this life and the next. Our spiritual nature is our core identity, the only identity that links us to all other human beings. Since we live in both the transitory and eternal realms at the same time, one of our greatest challenges is to keep our focus on the changeless essence within us and within everyone else.

"Piercing the veils of the seasons of life helps to give us perspective of the whole. From our winters, we come to know our springs better. Embracing each season of life, remembering that the season of loss is followed by a season of harvest, will help us see all the seasons as phases of one interconnected whole.

"The soul is the meeting ground between the human and the divine. This life, because of its vicissitudes, its wonders *and* its despair, prepares us for the life to come. To experience the unseen in the seen is a true test of vision. Pain is not less than joy, or even separate from it. Each struggle we endure is essential to our growth and renewal. A time will come when we will see beyond duality to the oneness that brought everything into existence."

Another student looked puzzled. "Do you mean that the despair and pain we see are not important?" she asked.

"Everything has its place and purpose," I answered. "The dynamic tension between all things is necessary. Joy cannot exist without sorrow. Sorrow creates a yearning for its opposite. The two forces continually wrestle with each other, yet neither wins forever. The season of doubt is followed by the season of certainty. Yet even certainty is subject to the return of doubt; but this is what confirms us in our understanding of who we really are. When we know from our own experience that joy and sorrow can embrace each other, creating a greater unity, we have found the heart of life. Our ongoing effort to become more conscious of this inherent oneness is the greatest adventure we can set out on."

I paused for a moment. As I looked around the circle, all the students were listening, patiently waiting. So I concluded with my innermost thoughts.

"Many years ago, as a curious child, a voice came to me telling me that someday I would know God. I did not know what that meant then. I have since found that the greatest pursuit of all is to seek the Unknowable.

"Revered in the myriad prayers, rituals, and sacred stories of all the diverse peoples, the Great Mystery, the Unseen, the Eternal, the Help in Peril, the Lord of all humanity, is known by a thousand names the world over. When we find a name expressing this Essence that appeals to our mind and touches our heart, we have found our connection to the one Spirit. More important than anything else is our conscious relationship with our Creator.

"The more we know of creation, and its eternal principles, the more there is to know. Only through reflections of the Divine, such as the workings of nature and the words of the prophets, can we come closer to knowing Ultimate Reality.

"In seeking to know the Infinite, we come to know more of the grand design that is life. This is how we also come to better understand our own potential, and our part in its unfolding.

"The only difference that matters in this life is the difference between the temporal and the everlasting. While all else around us is uncertain and inconsistent, only the Changeless remains constant and permanent. From the moonwalk comes a vision we all share, one of the clearest images of the Changeless: the heavens encircling the earth in a loving embrace. Remembering this often unites mind and soul, and one and all.

"We have all come from the same Source, and we are on a journey back to where we came from. The most sacred endeavors along our path are to love, to serve, and to remember. Could remembering where we have come from, who we are, what matters most in our life, and where we are going, be our most vital spiritual practice?

"Sometimes it takes so little on our part to bring so much our way from the spiritual realm. And sometimes we expend so little in giving so much to others; yet this is how we become instruments of grace ourselves.

"The brightest light is the one that passes from heart to heart. As a wave of love washing over all on earth, this light is awakening us all to a time of promise, a moment of destiny. Evolution is the journey toward the recognition of the oneness of all, and the holiness of everything.

"As we each move on, our thoughts of one another will grow into an echo of compassion; this is when we know we are never alone. Is the leaf, though it has its own branch, and its own call, ever not part of the tree? We, too, have grown together, as members of one human family, always part of the same sacred creation, and we shall remain part of each other as we continue on through the season of eternity. Our joy is in our lasting unity."

Notes & Afterthoughts

This formative time in my life provided the meaning for almost everything else that has followed. As Schopenhauer might say, this time has given me much of the text of my life while the next nearly fifty years have supplied the commentary on it. This just means that I was fortunate to have had a firm foundation upon which the evolution of my life was built.

These afterthoughts are meant to point to a few of the strong threads of continuity that still connect my life today with this earlier time. There is even a feeling of having come full circle with certain recent experiences connecting deeply with this time of my life.

SUMMER

The Hudson River Sloop *Clearwater* (p. 15), a 106' replica of the nineteenth-century vessels that carried cargo up and down the river, was founded by Pete Seeger and launched in 1969 to "save the river;" it has become America's Environmental Flagship, partnering with school and community groups, and in 2004 was named to the National Register of Historic Places for its groundbreaking role in the environmental movement. http://www.clearwater.org.

FALL

Walt Whitman's inspired and visionary expression of the self in relation to the universe (p. 28) is from "Song of Myself," *Leaves of Grass* (New York: Signet Classics, 2005).

William Blake's mystical juxtaposition of time and eternity (p. 29) is from "Auguries of Innocence" in *Poetry and Prose of William Blake*, edited by G. Keynes (New York: Viking, 1990).

C. G. Jung's inner-oriented autobiographical "personal myth" (p. 29) is from *Memories, Dreams, Reflections* (New York: Vintage Books, 1989).

Henry David Thoreau's wise words on how and why to live in the present and in harmony with nature (p. 31) are from *Walden* (New York: Signet Classics, 2004).

Ralph Waldo Emerson's thoughts on the reliance of divine providence (p. 31) are from "Self Reliance," in *The Portable Emerson*, edited by Carl Bode (New York: Penguin Classics, 1981).

Arlo Guthrie's song of his mystical experience, "Gabriel's Mother's Highway Ballad #16 Blues," (pp. 42–43) is found on his *Washington County* album. On the recorded version, he added the lines: "The sun come up while I wrote this song/Come on, children, come on/To remember me that it won't be long/Come on, children, come on."

WINTER

Joseph Campbell's pioneering work on comparative mythology describing the monomyth, or the pattern common to all the world's myths, *Hero with a Thousand Faces* (p. 49), was first published in 1949 by the Bollingen Foundation and is now a classic. My own book, *The Gift of Stories: Practical and Spiritual Applications of Autobiography, Life Stories and Personal Mythmaking* (Westport, CT: Greenwood Press, 1995), adapts the pattern of the monomyth to contemporary circumstances and settings for personal mythmaking.

Joseph Campbell's talk at Cooper Union (p. 51), "Schizophrenia—the Inward Journey," is published as chapter 10, in *Myths to Live By* (New York: Viking Press, 1972). His *The Masks of God, Vol. 4, Creative Mythology* was originally published by Viking Penguin, 1968.

The dream of the seven angels (pp. 60–64) is an allegorical illustration of how a sequence of manifestations of the Divine each conveys the essence of a universal, timeless spiritual truth. We know them as the Prophets of God, or the founders of the world's great religions: Krishna, Moses, Zoroaster, Buddha, Christ, Muhammad, and Bahá'u'lláh. Each one has initiated a new spiritual epoch causing a leap of consciousness for humanity.

The Bible of the World (p. 65), edited by Robert O. Ballou, was originally published by Viking Penguin in 1957, and is available now in a condensed form as *The Portable World Bible* (New York: Penguin, 1977).

The Religions of Man (p. 66) by Huston Smith, first published by Harper & Row in 1958 and by Perennial Library in 1965, is now available as *The World's Religions: Our Great Wisdom Traditions* (San Fransisco: HarperSanFrancisco, 1991).

The brochure (p. 67) I picked up at a sloop festival was my first introduction to the Bahá'í Faith. The idea that one God created one people with one continuously unfolding knowledge system (what we call religion) designed to shed more and more light upon the mysteries of the Creation and how to live harmoniously with it, was a natural for me; from my previous studies, it made intuitive sense immediately.

This conscious recognition intensified my search for common themes, principles, motifs, and archetypes in the world's religions. About three years later, while living in Spartanburg, South Carolina, I came in contact with the local Bahá'ís. After speaking with one about my interests in mythology and mysticism, he suggested I might be interested in reading Bahá'u'lláh's mystical work, The Seven Valleys. He was right. This was the first Bahá'í book I read, and it lead me to others. I soon became a Bahá'í, striving to incorporate the principles and teachings into my daily life.

For further reading, if you have areas of interest similar to mine, I'd suggest *The Bahá'í Faith: The Emerging Global Religion* (Wilmette, IL: Bahá'í Publishing, 2002) as an excellent overall introduction, as well as *Gleanings from the Writings of Bahá'u'lláh* (Wilmette, IL: Bahá'í Publishing, 2005), and *The Hidden Words* (Wilmette, IL: Bahá'í Publishing, 2002) for the essence of the writings of Bahá'u'lláh.

'Abdu'l-Bahá's *Some Answered Questions* (Wilmette, IL: Bahá'í Publishing Trust, 2014) and *The Promulgation of Universal Peace* (Wilmette, IL: Bahá'í

Publishing, 2012) address issues of spiritual development and the principles underlying the Bahá'í Faith.

Excellent topical compilations include *The Divine Art of Living* (Wilmette, IL: Bahá'í Publishing, 2006), and *The Reality of Man* (Wilmette, IL: Bahá'í Publishing, 2005), as well as *Bahá'u'lláh's Teachings on Spiritual Reality* (Riviera Beach, FL: Palabra Publications, 1996).

C.G. Jung's *Modern Man In Search of a Soul* (p. 69) was first published in 1933 by Houghton Miflin, and again in 1955 by Harcourt Brace.

SPRING

It was when I spoke with Joseph Campbell in more depth in his home in Greenwich Village (p. 73) that I became even more aware of the contemporary role of the ageless motifs and archetypes in our lives today. Linking more directly and specifically my own archetypal experiences to the pattern of the monomyth, and thinking of the process of the adventure that he described as departure-initiation-return in terms of beginning-muddle-resolution, enabled me to develop a contemporary version of this ageless pattern that could be applied to our own experiences today. This is what became chapter 5, "Universalizing Your Story: Personal Mythmaking," and chapter 6, "Merging Your Personal Myth with the Collective Myth," in my book, *The Gift of Stories.*

Plato's allegory of the cave (p. 75), a great lesson in going beyond the obvious, can be found in *The Republic* (New York: Penguin Classics, 2003).

Emerson's emphasis on the importance of the influence of nature on learning and creativity in "The American Scholar" (pp. 75–76) can be found in *The Portable Emerson* edited by Carl Bode.

Alfred North Whitehead's *The Aims of Education and Other Essays* (p. 76) was originally published in 1929 by The Free Press and reissued in 1967.

Black Elk's vision (p. 76), which consisted of hearing a sacred voice and coming to an understanding of his purpose in life, is in *Black Elk Speaks* by John G. Neihardt (New York: Pocket Books, 1972).

Arlo Guthrie's "Highway in the Wind" (pp. 80–81), used by permission of Appleseed Music, is on his *Alice's Restaurant* album.

Walt Whitman's "Song of the Open Road" (p. 81) comes from his poem "Song of Myself."

Laura Nyro's "Time and Love" (pp. 82–83) is used by permission of EMI/Blackwood Music and is on her album of the same title.

The Moody Blues' "The Balance," written by Graeme Edge, (pp. 84–85) is used by permission of Threshold Music and is on the album *Question of Balance.*

The course on folk-rock lyrics as poetry was the first college course I had taught (pp. 79–90), and the only time I taught that particular course. It was in many ways a unique, even magical, experience. It was also the basis for my first book, *Songs of the Open Road: Folk-Rock Lyrics and the Journey of the Hero* (New American Library, 1974).

The ongoing effort to connect with as many of my students as possible is a regular challenge. To have been given the opportunity to live the questions of my life, and to be able to speak of them, heart to heart with others, is my greatest blessing.

Without a doubt, the most important learning I received from my adventures of 1969, in the way I approach my teaching as well as my own life, has been an unfailing hope for the future, an undying hope for humanity. The awareness I came to then has given me a perspective on the world that can not be changed, no matter what, or how much, changes around me.

Two recent classroom moments have brought my teaching and learning experiences full circle, and right back to the closeness and honesty I felt from the discussions we had in this first college class I had ever taught. At the end of the spring 2007 semester graduate course in Human Development, we were considering non-Western classics, one of which was The Seven Valleys by Bahá'u'lláh. I was identifying some of the motifs of transformation that appear in this poetic, mystical expression of the stages of human development and how they compare to the motifs and archetypes found in Joseph Campbell's *Hero with a Thousand Faces.* We had earlier in the course covered my contemporary version of this in *The Gift of Stories,* that I had called the story model of adult development (beginning, muddle, resolution). I noted in particular the motif appearing in the Valley of Search: "At every step, aid from the Invisible Realm will attend him and the heat of his search will grow." I compared this to the motif of "supernatural aid" coming during the Departure phase of Campbell's monomyth.

Then a student spoke up, and said, "That seems so airy. I don't get how that can relate to real life at all."

After a thoughtful moment of silence, I said, "Maybe an example from my own life might help," and I told the story of how I was led to Joseph Campbell's *Hero With a Thousand Faces* for the first time while being drawn into a bookstore and then noticing a poster announcing his talk that evening a few blocks away, which I then attended (p. 51). I pointed out that the important part to that assistance coming to me is how I chose to respond to it. I also happened to mention that this experience is part of my memoir of 1969, describing a transformative time in my life.

A couple of weeks later, I read in this students' course journal, as the last paragraph of the final reflection on the course as a whole, "I really enjoyed Dr. Atkinson's self-disclosing story in our second to last class. It was nice to hear a personal story and it made me realize that 'The Seven Valleys' is not as 'out there' as I had thought. I appreciated his openness to share with us and look forward to his book coming out next year."

The second moment also occurred at the end of the spring 2007 semester, in my graduate course "Culture, Tradition, and Diversity." In the final class, as a way to wrap up our discussions on diversity, ethnicity, and multiple identities, I passed around a drawing from Guy Murchie's *The Seven Mysteries of Life* (New York: Mariner Books, 1999, ch.13) that illustrated the interrelatedness of the human family. It consisted of a "you" at the center surrounded by all the relatives we could ever have, parents, aunts, uncles, grandparents, and cousins, all extending outward from the center with arrows connecting everyone. It made it clear that, depending on how far back we go, we have over a thousand fifth cousins, over a million tenth cousins, and that every other person on this planet (of any ethnicity) is at least in the range of fiftieth cousin, making us all one human family.

I connected this to the role of counselors, educators, and helping professionals in bringing about a greater awareness of this fact. I said, "I believe that humanity will eventually become aware of its relatedness. As we've seen in this course, there are more and more scientific affirmations of this all the time. We may not see the full awareness of this in our lifetimes, but sometime in the future this understanding will be as clear to our descendants as our relationship to our 'blood' relatives is to us today. And this will change the way we relate to and behave towards each other."

Then a student asked, "Have you always been so optimistic?"

I reflected for a moment and said, "Always is a long time. I don't think children are really ready to always be optimistic. Most adolescents are probably not, either. But there comes a time in our lives, when certain kinds of experiences, combined with a maturity of thought, make it possible for us to always be optimistic, if we choose to be. There was a time in my life when I became conscious of certain things that gave me an understanding of where our collective evolution is leading us, even though there are times that feel like we are going backwards."

I mentioned that I was referring to this time in my life when I first came to the conscious awareness of—and belief in—the oneness of humanity, that nothing could ever change my mind enough again to cause me to go back to a previous way of viewing the world, and that this really does change forever the way I see and relate to others.

This abiding sense of hope was first given to me in my own experiences of 1969 and confirmed in everything I have since read from the Bahá'í writings. Obviously, the world has continued to change dramatically over the last five decades, and in ways that do not always seem for the better. Yet this core awareness of our oneness also gives us a vantage point from where we can recognize that a lifetime is but a moment in eternity, that our lives are links in an endless chain, connecting us to those who have come before us and to those who will come after us, and that what we each do in our lives contributes something to the next moment in eternity.

Another recent event has brought my adventures of 1969 full circle in a different way. In late May of 2007, I realized the fulfillment of the end of my dream at the monastery (pp. 63–64) on my Bahá'í pilgrimage to the Holy Land. Upon hallowed ground in the valley of Acre, and on nearby

Mt. Carmel, in Haifa, Israel, I walked in the footsteps of the prophets, experienced directly a spiritual heritage common to all, and saw the reality of the evolution of religion with my own eyes.

With humbleness and devotion, I sought to envision the essence of what earlier pilgrims may have seen, to meditate in the tranquility of these holy places, and to absorb as much of the spiritual energy there as possible.

Approaching the golden-domed Shrine of the Báb, I couldn't help but be aware that all around me were beautifully landscaped terraces, exquisite gardens, verdant trees, plants, colorful flowers of sweet scents, and fountains of flowing water, a veritable paradise, existing solely for the glory of the Creator.

In the Shrine of Bahá'u'lláh, with a revivifying breeze blowing over me, in silent supplication, overwhelmed by the undeniable spirit of holiness, my heart was moved with a tenderness never before known, and my deepest prayer flowed forth.

And then in the prison cell where Bahá'u'lláh and others suffered such deprivation and indignity, I heard only words of comfort and confirmation, which will sustain me through all times: Your dream is real. Separation is an illusion. Humanity *is* one, and all realms of Creation are one.

*"More than ever today when the world
is facing such a crisis of bewilderment and unrest,
must we stand firm in faith
seeking that which binds together instead of tearing apart.
To those searching for light, the Bahá'í Teachings
offer a star which will lead them to deeper understanding,
to assurance, peace, and good will with all men."*

Queen Marie of Romania, 1936